C000272272

The Buxton Stage

Colin Wells

The Buxton Stage

with drawings by Rose Shawe-Taylor

Millrace

First published in Great Britain in 1998 by
Millrace
2a Leafield Road, Disley
Cheshire SK12 2JF

ISBN: 1 902173 02 3

Printed and bound in Great Britain by
Bookcraft (Bath) Ltd, Midsomer Norton, Avon

Contents

The Opera House at Buxton is a gem of a theatre - a marvel of Edwardian architectural design. Why should the town, 1,000 feet up in the hills, have such a magnificent theatre? The answer lies in the fortunes of Buxton as an inland resort, a spa. Its history has been first and foremost associated with the taking of the waters. For hundreds of years, the town's unique mineral water has attracted visitors seeking a cure for their ailments or simply coming to the town for a course of water treatment and a period of rest. The Romans used the waters for medicinal purposes and relaxation and the thermal springs saw royal patronage by Mary, Queen of Scots, during her imprisonment in the Hall in the 1570s. Buxton's baths were developed in the eighteenth century in an attempt to rival the developing facilities on offer at the Somerset watering place of

Bath and the town saw its greatest period of expansion in the latter half of the nineteenth century.

Entertainment has always been an important attraction for the visitor. To arrive at the reasons for the existence of the Opera House, we have first to describe something of the history of entertainment in Buxton. Investment in the Opera House came as a result of many years of theatrical provision, so what this book seeks to do is chronicle the history of theatre in Buxton, culminating in the history of Buxton's jewel, the Opera House, right through to the present day. How did it come to be built? Who designed it? Who trod the boards there? All these questions are addressed and for the first time research has been conducted into the technical developments at the theatre since its 1979 restoration. As the reader will see, Buxton has upheld a fine tradition of theatrical appreciation throughout its past and, with this in mind, let us (with apologies to Dylan Thomas)

begin at the beginning.

Overture

Health seekers visiting Buxton throughout the ages typically entered a prescribed water and dietary regime dictated by the town's water physicians. This treatment took place in the daytime, when the baths were open to the public. There were those who chose not to indulge in the treatment and for them traditional daytime pastimes were available, such as shooting, horse racing and cock fighting. Dr John Jones, writing in 1572, tells us of 'bowling in allayes, shooting at garden butts', and a game for the ladies known as 'Troule in Madame', in which the participants

> *'may have in the end of a benche, eleven holes made, intoo the which to troule pummetes, or bowles of leade, bigger, little or mean, or also of copper, tynne, woode, either violent or softe, after their own discretion.'*[1]

Bowling was on offer from 1695 onwards, when the landlord of the Hall, Cornelius White, had a bowling green constructed on his grounds. White also had a pack of hounds kennelled at the Hall which were used for hunting in the surrounding countryside. Horse racing took place on the Barms (Fairfield Common) from 1821-1840 and cockfighting had taken place in Buxton from the middle sixteenth century, more latterly at a cockpit on the site of today's Wesley Chapel on the Market Place.[2]

When the daytime activities were over, and after the baths were closed, the evenings were left free and both visitors and health seekers would have been seeking amusement and entertainment. During the Georgian and Victorian periods we know that the Assembly Room at the Crescent was much frequented by wealthy visitors for balls and card games. Additional facilities were provided, with the building of a billiard hall at the bottom of Hall Bank in the early nineteenth century, but what else was on offer?

One of the most enduring forms of entertainment throughout the ages is the art of acting. The portrayal of stories through theatrical and musical performances remains popular today but was considerably more important as a form of entertainment in days gone by, before the introduction of television and radio which do so much to distract modern man and woman from live entertainment. Music and drama have been performed in Buxton not only in theatres but also in front rooms, public halls and hotels.

There is anecdotal evidence of the existence of an early Buxton theatre in Church Street, near to St Anne's Church. The historian Ernest Axon,[3] however, gives little credence to it and suggests that a more likely site for a theatre was a barn on the land now occupied by the Devonshire Royal Hospital, which could have been in operation as early as 1776. Quite why Axon is so dismissive of the Church Street theatre is not made clear in his writings, particularly as, as we shall see later, a famous comedy actor and an actor/manager of a Buxton theatre were both buried in St Anne's churchyard.

The first documented evidence of a theatre describes a building at the corner of Spring Gardens and Hardwick Street. The date of its erection is not known precisely but it was probably in operation by about 1784. By all accounts not an architectural masterpiece, the theatre was variously described as:

'A mean dirty, boarded, thatched house, and can hold but few people.' (Colonel Byng, June 1790[4])

'A mean, ill constructed, thatched building.'
(George Frederick Cooke, a brilliant though reputedly drunken acting member of the Buxton Company[5])

'What a mean building! But for the words Pit and Boxes over the door, it would be mistaken for a barn. We found it much prettier within; it was newly painted, and the performers were better than we could have expected on such a stage; some indeed were excellent in their line.'
(Unnamed lady writing to her sister whilst lodging at Hall Bank on August 19th 1810[6])

'Its outside appearance is mean in the extreme; but within it is well fitted up, and may be pronounced a pretty little theatre.' (Jewitt, 1811[7])

Apart from the universal usage of the adjective 'mean' what can these descriptions tell us about the Spring Gardens theatre? It was obviously small and contemporary engravings show a barn-like building, with its gable end facing north, which could well be the theatre. It had a pit and boxes and was probably better fitted out in the interior than externally. Gas lighting did not arrive in Buxton until 1851 and therefore the auditorium and stage would have been candlelit. The writings of Robert Elliston (1774-1831), actor and theatre manager, inform us that a few stage footlamps fitted with tallow candles lit the whole theatre. It was not the practice in theatres at this time to darken the auditorium during a performance, so spectators were clearly visible to other members of the audience, which was not a minor consideration for the social elite.[8] The pit was composed of a line of hurdles which were designed to keep the feet of the audience dry during wet weather as the theatre was liable to flooding. The company was small in number and of venerable age, with the exception of two urchins. They had precious little in the way of scenery and indeed seem to have been restricted to a double-sided backdrop which had been turned so often over the years as to be nearly unrecognisable.[9]

The first known manager of the theatre was a Mr Welch and both he and John Ferrizer obtained licences for theatrical performances in Buxton and

Bakewell in 1788. The theatre company consisted of players who were considered by Jewitt to be 'far above mediocrity'[10] and were often augmented during the bathing season by more distinguished actors from London. The theatre was only open during the bathing season (1st July to the end of October) and then only three nights a week. Performances commenced at 6.00 pm and could go on until midnight or even later. If the surviving collection of early theatre playbills is an accurate representation of what was on offer, it seems that the Buxton audiences preferred comedy to tragedy. The format of an evening's entertainment at the theatre followed a pretty set pattern which featured firstly the main entertainment of the evening, followed by a comic song or dance, and finished almost invariably with a farce. An example of one such programme of 1792 appears opposite.

The Mr Kane featured in the playbill, playing the part of 'Old Cockney', was John Kane (1741-99), a comedy actor from Dublin, who unfortunately died in Buxton at the age of 58 after eating hemlock which he had gathered, mistakenly believing it to be horseradish. Kane's grave is still to be seen in St Anne's churchyard and is in a poor state, despite

BY DESIRE OF HER GRACE THE

DUTCHESS OF RUTLAND

BUXTON THEATRE.

On SATURDAY Evening August the 25th. 1792. will be performed,
A COMEDY called. THE

BUSY BODY.

Sir George Airy, Mr. FAIRBAIRN,
Sir Francis Gripe, Mr. GRANT,
Sir Jealous Traffic, Mr. DAVIS,
Charles, Mr. NELSON
Whisper, Mr. WENTWORTH,
Butler, Mr. MAYCOCK.
Marplot, (the Busy Body.) Mr. MARTIN.

Miranda, Mrs. NELSON,
Isabinda Mrs. HARDING,
Scentwell, Mrs. FAIRBAIRN,
Patch, Mrs. WENTWORTH,

End of Act the Third, Collins's favorite SONG of

"The West Country Clown"

BY Mr. HARDING,

End of the PLAY,

The "HOBBIES of the TIMES" by Mr. HARDING,

To which will be added, a Musical FARCE, called, THE

R O M P.

Watty Cockney, Mr. MARTIN,
Capt. Sightly, Mr. HARDING,
Old Cockney, Mr KANE,—Servant, Mr. MAYCOCK.
Old Barnacle, Mr. DAVIS.

Priscilla, Tomboy, (the Romp.) Mrs. WENTWORTH,
La-Blond, Mrs MARTIN,—Quashaba, Miss, FAIRBAIRN,
Penelope. Mrs FAIRBAIRN

BOXES: 3s. PIT, 2s GALLERY, 1s.

To begin exactly a quarter before six, and finish at Nine or soon after.

TICKETS to be had at Bott's and Moore's Circulating Library's, of the Waiters at the Hall, both Hotel's, and all the Inns being restored by the Victorian comedian J L Toole in 1889.

Another name, S W Ryley, was associated with the theatre from possibly as early as 1787. Ryley served as both actor and actor/manager for the Buxton company. Ernest Axon gives us some interesting details of Ryley's financial situation at the end of the 1787 season:

'An incident on the last day of this Buxton season shows that Ryley was by no means in funds on the completion of his season's contract. An attorney to whom he owed money for work done in another town got a warrant for Ryley's arrest for debt. The Sheriff's officer for whom the warrant was committed kept the 'Black Horse' (probably a disguised name) in Buxton, and forged a message asking Ryley to meet the manager of the Bath Theatre there. Without pausing to think of the likelihood of a manager being at such a low public [house] Ryley went there and was told by the landlady what the business was. Before she could announce his arrival he flung her to the further end of the room, locked her in, and rushed off. At the 'White Hart' the Manchester coach, in which he had already booked his seat, was standing. Into it

he jumped, and crouching down was hidden from view for ten minutes, when venturing to peep out he was seen by one of the Sheriff's men who was in the road.

Promptly Ryley opened the coach door on the other side and rushed into the 'White Hart' and locked himself in a lower room, through the closed windows of which he had a heated argument with the officer. The shouting attracted a crowd and Ryley was advised to pay the debt or surrender, to which he replied 'I cannot pay the debt, I have no bail to give, and I will not be arrested if I can avoid it.' The amount of the debt was only £10. Mrs Wheeldon, the landlady, now came to his assistance, fastened all the outer doors, and invited Ryley upstairs to a more comfortable room. Then a gentleman offered the use of his horse, in exchange for the seat Ryley had booked on the coach. The horse proved to be no racer either uphill or down, and when Ryley was four miles from Buxton he found that he was being followed by a much better mounted horseman.

At this moment a huge waggon almost blocked the road and in his haste in passing it Ryley pushed the waggoner into the ditch. This annoyed the waggoner, who, taking the second rider to be one of the first rider's party, blocked the road and with his whip was intending to repay the damage he had received. The delay enabled Ryley to get to Whaley Bridge and Cheshire twenty yards ahead of his pursuer. He was safe there, for the sheriff's officer had no powers of arrest outside his own county of Derby. Ryley, bearing no ill will, treated him to a bowl of punch.' [11]

Following Ryley as Buxton's theatre manager was Mr Thornhill who, by all accounts, was an indefatigable man, both in respect of his post as manager and in the creation of his family, which numbered ten children. The whole family was involved with the company and Mrs and the Misses Thornhill regularly appear on the handbills of the time.

It was during Thornhill's period of management that Buxton received a visit from one of the country's most noted actors, Edmund Kean (1787-1833). Kean had not visited the town with any intention of performing but was persuaded to do so by Thornhill who offered him half of the receipts if he would play his greatest part, that of Richard III. Kean consented and there was a packed house for the performance, for which he actually refused payment.

Jewitt, writing in 1811, indicated that the lease of the theatre was nearly expired and that it was hoped that the Duke of Devonshire would build another and more comfortable theatre in the village. It may seem unusual from today's point of view to expect the Duke of Devonshire to supply the inhabitants with a theatre but this was very much the attitude of the Buxton villagers of the time. However, the fifth Duke died in 1811 and the question of a replacement theatre was left in the air. The Spring Gardens theatre was closed or demolished about 1829. It is likely that the town was without a theatre for a few years afterwards, but entertainment was still to be had in Buxton with the opening of a new Promenade and Music Room in the Crescent in 1828.

The question of a new theatre was pursued further by the Duke of Devonshire's agent, Philip Heacock, who was very aware of the need to attract visitors to the town by providing improved facilities. The beginning of the nineteenth century had seen an increase in the popularity of the seaside holiday as opposed to the inland spa. Heacock strongly promoted the medical advantages of a visit to Buxton and was astute enough to realise that the changing fashions would be ignored to the estate's detriment. His influence seemed to find favour with the Duke and a new theatre was erected at the foot of Hall Bank, opposite the Old Hall, in 1833. The expenditure of £445.2.5d is recorded under repairs for the 'New Theatre' in the accounts book of the Duke's agent for the year ending Ladyday 1833,[12] and playbills of 1834 are all headed 'New Theatre'. A block layout of this theatre is shown on the 1848 tithe map but unfortunately no clear image of it exists, despite several engravings which show the general area. None of them give a satisfactory view of the theatre, which was somewhat awkwardly situated behind a house and shop on land which is today occupied by Broad Walk.

Despite this, it would probably be safe to assume that the 'new' theatre was a considerable improvement on the theatre in Spring Gardens. It is referred to by Rhodes as:

> *'a small place, but neat and convenient within, and occupied during the season by a very respectable company of comedians.'* [13]

The tithe map shows the theatre standing behind the shop and next door to the billiard room, and gives it a land area of six perches (thirty-three square yards). There are many ways in which this area could be configured but, if we are to assume that the building took the shape of a standard rectangle, it is possible to enclose that area in a building measuring twenty by fifteen feet. This total area would need to include stage, auditorium and presumably some space for costume changing, etc, so it is not difficult to imagine how small it would seem compared to our modern theatres. Like the Spring Gardens theatre, it would have been lit by candle or oil lamps but may later have been gaslit, which would have enabled the stage lighting to be more directional, allowing the auditorium to be darkened during a performance. Interestingly, the introduction of gas lighting into theatres doubled the number of theatres destroyed by fire throughout the country.[14]

As with its predecessor, the theatre was only open for about three months during the summer season. In the autumn of 1833 the New Theatre played host to the famous violinist, Nicolo Paganini (1782-1840), when the house was packed, despite raised admission charges.

The Thornhill family remained heavily involved with the new theatre and playbills show the family members making up the cast of several productions. One such playbill, dated Saturday September 6th 1834, is headed: 'for the benefit of Mr Meadows, of the Theatre Royal, Covent Garden, the musical play *Rob Roy: or Auld Lang Syne.'*

Drinkwater Meadows was an eminent actor of his time and his appearance must have been quite an acquisition for the Buxton Company. This Saturday performance was the last of three appearances, with Meadows playing the part of Bailie Nicol Jarvie. The main piece was followed by a comic song from Mr Weston and the evening was concluded in the usual pattern by a farce entitled *Illustrious Stranger or Buried Alive* in which Mr Meadows took the part of Benjamin Bowball.

Prices at the new theatre remained unchanged, with boxes costing 3 shillings (15p), pit 2s (10p) and gallery 1s (5p). Cheaper rates (boxes 2s, pit 1s 6d (13p) and gallery 6d (3p)) could be had if one was prepared to enter the theatre at the end of the third act, just in time to see the farce. These prices were relatively high compared to the average wages of the time and probably meant that only the higher wage earners could consider using the facility. Generally speaking, a labourer of the 1840s earned in the region of 14s (70p) a week and those who were totally unskilled would have earned several shillings less than that. Railway navvies could earn from 15s (75p) a week in a poor year to 24s in a good year, which was considered a relatively high wage.[15]

Music for the theatrical performances was provided by the Duke's band or selected musicians from it. The same band also played in the Assembly and Music Rooms and outside the Crescent, sporting grey uniforms. A Mr Deakin, who played the cornet, features on some of the playbills and it is thought that he appeared on stage as and when necessary.

The Buxton company gave a performance of a local play, *Poole the Outlaw,* on August 15th 1837 which drew on the tradition and legend of an early occupant of Buxton's show cave, Poole's Cavern.

The theatre was demolished in 1854 after a relatively brief existence. The Buxton Estate Accounts at Chatsworth for the year ending Ladyday (March 25th) 1855 include an entry for 'stone from the old theatre', which confirms that the building had been demolished by that time.[16] Why the theatre was taken down after such a short time is not known but a clue might lie in the Chatsworth accounts which in 1851 show the tenant of the theatre, John Capel, to be a bad payer and in debt to the estate to the tune of £20.[17] An accumulation of such debts may have brought about the closure of the theatre or the building may have simply been demolished to make way for the construction of Broad Walk, which commenced in 1861. The site of the theatre was used to build the first three houses of Broad Walk, known as Cavendish Villas, erected for Mr G F Barnard, a wine and spirit merchant in town.[18]

So, once again, the town was without a purpose-built theatre and this was to remain the case for many years to follow.

References

1 Jones, Dr John: *The Benefit of the Auncient Bathes of Buckstones.* 1572

2 Axon, Ernest, FSA: *Historical Notes on Buxton, its Inhabitants and Visitors.* Paper XVIII

3 Axon, Ernest: op cit. Paper X. Theatres and Actors of Old Buxton

4 Colonel Byng, later Viscount Torrington: *The Torrington Diaries, 1781-1794.* 4 Volumes. Edited by C Bruyn Andrews. Barnes & Noble Inc. New York. Methuen & Co Ltd. London

5 Axon, Ernest: op cit. Paper X

6 Jewitt: *A History of Buxton.* 1811
7 Jewitt: op cit. 1811
8 Wickham, Glynne: *A History of the Theatre*. Phaidon Press. 1992. (2nd edition)
9 Raymond, George. *Memoirs of Robert William Elliston, Comedian, 1774-1810.* John Mortimer. London. 1844
10 Jewitt: op cit. 1811
11 Axon, Ernest: op cit. Paper X
12 Philip Heacock's Accounts for Year Ending Ladyday 1833. Devonshire Buxton collection, Chatsworth
13 Rhodes: Derbyshire Tourists Guide. 1837
14 Wickham: op cit. 1992
15 Miles, Joyce: *The rise of Suburban Exeter and the Naming of its Streets and Houses c 1801-1907.* Leicester PhD. 1990. p. 144
16 Buxton Estate Accounts, year ending Ladyday 1855. Devonshire Collection, Chatsworth
17 Buxton Estate Accounts. Arrears due at Ladyday 1851. Devonshire Collection, Chatsworth
18 Langham, M & Wells, C. *The Architect of Victorian Buxton.* Derbyshire Library Service. 1996

Beginners on Stage

Despite the absence of a theatre, musical and dramatic performances continued to take place at the Assembly Room in the Crescent and in the Courthouse on George Street. On June 29th 1861 the Clavert Theatre Company of Manchester applied to the Devonshire Buxton Estate to hire the ballroom for use as a theatre for three nights a week for a total of twelve nights. The ballroom was leased to the company for two shillings per evening, including gas, but was to be given up at the end of the first week if it proved to be a nuisance to the house.[1] In October 1871 a new theatre was established in the disused Independent Chapel at the bottom of the hill leading on to Spring Gardens (now Holker Road) but the venture proved to be short-lived. Grandly named the Theatre Royal, it opened for its first performance on October 7th 1871 with an evening of drama, comedy and farce. The theatre

appears to have closed down later in the month after the manager of the establishment, Mr Henry Mandeville, absconded, taking all he could lay his hands on and leaving his players unpaid.

The sixth Duke of Devonshire died in 1858, leaving debts for his successor. The seventh Duke decided to use his existing capital to generate more income and reduce the regular financial outgoings which were becoming a drain on the estate. The maintenance of the Hall gardens, the Serpentine and the expense of the town band fell into this category and he decided to hand over the upkeep of these facilities to a company which could develop the area and make it profitable. He put forward a proposal at a rent audit dinner in November 1867 to donate twelve acres of land in the Hall gardens and bear half the cost of building a large summer house or 'winter garden' on the land if a company could be formed to take responsibility for its future maintenance. Consequently the Buxton Improvements Company was formed and its first meeting was held on December 4th 1869, chaired by the proprietor of the *Buxton Advertiser*, John Cumming Bates. The memorandum and articles of association were submitted to the Register of Joint Stock Companies and received the status of a limited company on March 5th 1870. The company's capital of £12,000 was raised by the issue of 2,400 shares at £5 each and the shareholders were largely local business people.

The company employed the architect, Edward Milner, to design and build the iron and glass pavilion or winter garden and to design and lay out the gardens. The building incorporated a central hall which was to be used for concerts by the town band and a covered promenade running west and east of the hall, giving the building a total length of 400 feet. It was completed in 1871 and shows clearly the influence of Sir Joseph Paxton, under whom Milner had served as a student. The gardens were also landscaped by Milner and his son, Henry Ernest, using an undulating style of landscaping, creating areas of light and shade in the park. The river Wye was dammed in several places so as to create differing water levels and falls and the completed pleasure grounds were opened to the public on May 11th 1871.

The Pavilion Gardens were a great success from the beginning and large numbers of visitors paid the admission charge in order to sample the facilities on offer. The complex offered two promenading areas: outside the pavilion in good weather conditions and inside the building in less fair conditions. To walk the whole length of the pavilion building, it was necessary to pass through the central hall where the band concerts were held. The regular theatrical and musical performances were very well attended, often to the point of overcrowding. This became a source of irritation to the promenaders and vice versa to the concert goers, who had to put up with a constant stream of people pushing through the hall during a performance. The central hall was only seventy feet square and it was a far from unusual sight to witness people sitting on the stone sills outside the building to catch a glimpse of the orchestral concert. This situation could not be allowed to continue and as early as 1872 pressure was being applied to the Improvements Company to do something to alleviate the problem. As a short-term measure, the company sought to decrease the congestion by raising the price of a weekly admission ticket from two shillings (10p) to two shillings and sixpence (13p) and from five shillings (25p) to seven shillings (35p). It is not known whether these increases actually took place and, if they did, whether they achieved their object but pressure certainly continued on the company to find a permanent solution.

In November 1872 the directors of the Improvements Company enlisted the help of the local architect, Robert Rippon Duke, to design an extension to the pavilion building which would provide sufficient space to house the orchestra and its audience. Duke made several suggestions by which the building could be converted to accommodate the extra visitors, including the widening of the pavilion corridors, enlargement of the central hall and the provision of extra space for cloakrooms, etc. However, it was obvious that the architect preferred his alternative suggestion of building a completely new concert hall at the west end of the pavilion, large enough to hold 2,000 people, at a cost of £6,000. This was the option eventually chosen by the company and work on the hall commenced, with the laying of the foundation stone on December 30th 1875 by the chairman of the company, Dr W H Robertson, physician at the Devonshire Hospital and much respected townsman.

Duke's design was bold and adventurous considering that he had not tackled a project of such complexity before. In keeping with the existing pavilion building, the concert hall was built with glass and ironwork. The building was opened to the public on August 30th 1876 by the Duke of Devonshire and the first concert in the new hall took place, featuring the town band under the leadership of pianist and conductor, Julian Adams. The evening was completed by a giant firework display which was somewhat marred by rain.

The hall remains today and is octagonal in shape, with a diameter of over 100 feet, and is surmounted by a dome 68 feet in height, with side windows to let in light from the ceiling. The dome interior is of pitched pine and the centre of the dome holds a 'sunlight' gas burner which lit the building from above in the evenings. Much doubt had been expressed in the *Buxton Advertiser* during the building of the hall, particularly about the acoustical qualities of a large domed roof, but all such doubts were dispelled upon its opening when it was found that the hall has surprisingly good acoustic properties. The cost of building the concert hall in 1876 was £8,000, which compares rather favourably with the reroofing of the dome recently at a cost of over £31,000.[2]

Buxton now had a new concert hall and much improved facilities for orchestral concerts and recitals, etc, but it still did not have a theatre. Public demand for a theatre must have been recognised by the Improvements Company and in 1887 the directors were discussing the possibility of providing an 'additional large room for general entertainments'. The word *theatre* could not be used during these discussions since the chairman of the company, Dr Robertson, thought theatre to be rather a vulgar business. The terms of the Memorandum of Association of the company did not permit the erection of such a building and it was necessary to reconstruct the company with extended powers which would allow for the construction of the new building and any others that it might choose to erect. Consequently, the Buxton Improvements Company ceased to exist on March 27th 1888 and was replaced by a new company named the Buxton Gardens Company.[3] The company secretary at that time was John Willoughby, a man who worked hard to secure the new theatre and, subsequently, the Opera House.

With its increased powers, the reformed company could proceed with its plans for a 'large room for general entertainments'. The local architect, William Radford Bryden, was chosen to design the building. Bryden had bought the practice of Buxton's prime architect, Robert Rippon Duke, when he 'retired' in 1883. He soon established his reputation as a more than competent architect when he designed his first significant Buxton building, the Union Club in 1886 (known to us now as The Old Clubhouse). He went on to build more of the town's more impressive architecture, including The Hawthorns, Burlington Road (1896), Milnthorp Homes (1905) and Buxton Hospital (1912).

The choice of site for the new theatre is puzzling. It stands behind the Pavilion building, with its roof structure clearly visible from the Gardens promenade and totally spoiling the airy and light impression which was originally intended for this building. The site was occupied by glasshouses and potting sheds which needed to be resited at no small cost to the company. The insistence of the Gardens Company chairman on calling the building by any other name than *theatre* caused some sarcasm in the local press, more particularly when, as the building approached completion, they had to apply for a theatrical licence. The licence was applied for on

July 6th 1889 and, after an inspection of the building by local magistrates, was granted on July 20th. The theatre was completed later that year and was opened for its first public performance on August 12th 1889. The company did not want an opening ceremony but the moment was given recognition by the actor John Lawrence Toole (1830-1906) who made a small speech before the commencement of *The Don*, a play in which he played the lead role.[4]

The name chosen for the theatre, in deference to Dr Robertson, was the Entertainment Stage but it quickly became known as the New Theatre and later the Pavilion Theatre. It was a substantial improvement on all its predecessors and had a two-level auditorium seating 850 people, a stage with somewhat limited space in the wings and dressing rooms in the basement. The ticket office was at the entrance from St John's Road and, although the north facing facade is not particularly inspiring, it is worthwhile to study the stonework of the 'Dutch' gables, which are quite intricately carved with stage motifs. Gables of this type are a notable feature in much of Bryden's architectural designs.

The Pavilion Theatre was managed by John Willoughby (1838-1916) who was overall manager of the Pavilion Gardens and secretary of the Buxton Gardens Company. The theatre hosted a full programme of plays throughout the season, including a three-night presentation beginning on Thursday August 26th 1897:

'By Mr Abud's Exceptionally Powerful London Company, With an exact reproduction of the magnificent scenery, uniforms etc, from the St James' Theatre, London, by arrangement with Mr George Alexander, in the phenomenally successful play - ***The Prisoner of Zenda'***

The famous play by Brandon Thomas, *Charley's Aunt,* was presented at the theatre for three nights beginning August 22nd 1898 and the grand Christmas pantomime version of *Robinson Crusoe* began a one-week run commencing February 21st 1898. A glance at the programme for this panto suggests a great many scene changes took place during the production. There were twelve scenes:

1 Davy Jones' Locker; 2 Port of Hull; 3 Deck of the 'Octopus'; 4 The open ocean; 5 Sea coast on desert island ; 6 Another part of the island; 7 Exterior of Crusoe's hut; 8 Interior of Crusoe's hut; 9 An apartment in the Palace; 10 Grand banquet in the Palace; 11 A street; 12 Beautiful village scene (winter)

Not much rest in this show for the backstage staff! In September 1902 the theatre was honoured by a visit from the famous acting partnership of Mr and Mrs Kendal who stayed for a two-night production of *The Elder Miss Blossom.*[5]

The theatre remained financially buoyant throughout this period and the *Buxton Advertiser* congratulated the secretary of the Gardens Company on the excellent bookings he had made during the year 1901. The profit made from the theatre for that year was £2,401, which was sufficient to pay a dividend to the shareholders of nearly seven per cent on the share capital of £35,827.[6] With such a sound financial footing it might appear that the last thing the town needed was another theatre but, only two years after the announcement of such healthy profits, we had one: the Opera House.

References

1 'Buxton Office 1856'. Devonshire Collection, Chatsworth. A large suede-covered bound volume with red label 'Buxton Office 1856'
2 For a more detailed description of the building of the Concert Hall see Langham & Wells: *The Architect of Victorian Buxton*. Derbyshire Library Service. 1996. pp 77-9
3 Annual Report of the Buxton Improvements Company. March 27th 1888
4 Axon, Ernest, FSA: *Historical Notes on Buxton, its Inhabitants and Visitors.* Paper X
5 *Buxton Advertiser,* September 17th 1902
6 *Buxton Advertiser,* December 27th 1902

Curtain Up

By the turn of the century the Gardens Company obviously felt the need to create a larger and more comfortable theatre. A special meeting of the company on October 7th 1901 decided upon the expenditure of £25,000 (exclusive of land) for the building of a new theatre and the reconstruction of the main entrance to the Pavilion Gardens. Some consideration had been given to the conversion of the Pavilion Theatre but the conclusion reached was that only a completely new, purpose-built theatre could provide the required facilities.[1]

The company chose the prolific architect, Frank Matcham (1854-1920), to design the new theatre. Matcham was born in Newton Abbot, Devon, and trained under one of the foremost theatre architects of the day, Jethro T Robinson, the designer of the Theatre Royal, Margate, and the major reconstruction of the Old Vic Theatre. Matcham married

Robinson's daughter, Maria, and after the death of Robinson in 1877 took over the architectural business with an office in London. Robinson had been involved in the rebuilding of the Elephant and Castle Theatre in Southwark at the time of his death and Matcham immediately took over the project, seeing the building successfully through to completion.

The choice of Matcham was an inspired one and the town should consider itself lucky that he could find the time in his busy schedule to build such a theatre in our remote province. To call Matcham prolific is no exaggeration and can be clearly demonstrated by the fact that, of the 400 or so theatres built between 1880 and 1912, Matcham was responsible for at least 150 of them. Taking these figures and dividing them by the years in which he was active, he was producing an average of eight theatres a year, a huge achievement by any standards.[2]

Nationally, the years between the 1880s and 1914 saw a surge in theatre building, fuelled by a rapidly growing population with comparably increased incomes who were seeking entertainment. By the turn of the century virtually all the cities and large towns in the country could boast a Matcham theatre and some of them two. He was renowned for the speedy and punctual completion of his building work and the high quality of his design. In many circumstances he was asked to design and build a new theatre in a space left by the demolition of an existing building in what would appear to be a hopelessly small landspace but the ingenuity of the man enabled him to fit a 'quart into a pint pot' in all but the most difficult cases. Amongst the many theatres which he designed are the Grand Theatre, Blackpool (1894), the Grand Opera House, Belfast (1895), the London Hippodrome (1900), and the London Palladium (1910).

Matcham designed his theatres to make the audience feel entertained even before the show began and hence his interiors, although using very different styles in each case, are generally very embellished and lack formal restraint. This caused him to receive criticism from the purists in theatre design.[3] The author of the three-volume *Modern Opera Houses and Theatres* (1896-8), Edwin Sachs, shows his disdain for Matcham's style by including scant mention of Matcham in his work other than his name in the list of original subscribers to the book. The final paragraph of his coverage of Matcham's

Grand Theatre, Islington (1883) reads:

> *'Finally, to those who may feel some astonishment that this theatre should find a place in these volumes, I would point out the fact of its being the forerunner of the suburban theatre gives it an importance which cannot be overestimated. Whatever may be the defects of the site and plan, when we remember that the building was designed as recently as 1882, there is much in the arrangement which cannot fail to receive attention from those interested in theatre construction.'*[4]

Matcham's most productive years covered the transition of popularity from music hall to variety theatre through to purpose-built theatres, and the design of his theatres throughout the period 1880-1912 reflect these changes. Despite such implied criticism from his peers, he understood the nature of the people who attended his theatres and designed them with their needs in mind. The working man could visit one of his theatres and at once encounter an Aladdin's cave of an interior, making him feel in a special place where, just perhaps, magical things could happen.

The contractor for the Opera House was Mr Vickers of Nottingham. It was decided to build the new theatre on land which already belonged to the company and in a prominent position next to the main entrance of the Pavilion Gardens. This necessitated moving the east wing of the conservatory building some distance closer to the river in order to site the theatre within the existing land boundary. Early in November 1901 the curator of the Pavilion Gardens, Adam Hogg, and his assistant, Mr West, commenced work on widening the terrace towards the river so that the building could be repositioned.[5] The work of digging out the foundations for the Opera House began in early February 1902 and reputedly took four months to conclude before the actual building could be started.[6]

The new frontages of both the Pavilion Gardens and the new Opera House could be seen in October 1902 as the buildings began to appear over the hoardings which had hitherto hidden the work from public view. What could be seen was felt by all to be most favourable and work on the gardens entrance increased in pace. The new entrance was officially opened on Wednesday November 19th 1902 by Mr J H Lawson, who was the first to pass through the turnstile.[7] Parts of the theatre had been built up to roof level by the end of November and the building works received a visit from the Duke and Duchess of Devonshire in January 1903. Speculation abounded in the town when it was announced that the theatre was to be visited by King Edward VII and Queen Alexandra but in the event the king contracted influenza and the visit was cancelled. 1903 was a busy year for Matcham (although no busier than most years for this workaholic of a man) and along with the Opera House he was actively engaged with the construction of the London Coliseum, the Manchester Hippodrome, Kings, Glasgow, Shepherds Bush Empire, Olympia, Liverpool and the Marlborough Theatre, Islington, all of which he visited on a regular basis.[8]

The scaffolding in front of the building was removed in April 1903 and the complete exterior of the theatre was revealed for the first time. The theatrical newspaper *The Era* makes it clear that the new theatre was going to be something special:

'In order to make room for the new theatre, it was found necessary to reconstruct the entrance to the Gardens in a new position. The new entrance is

formed at the side of the theatre, the public entering by a large centre opening (protected by an iron glass shelter) and by two dwarf stone towers with coloured glass domes. The whole forms practically a crescent with a wide carriage drive in the front and the whole has a very commanding appearance.

The new theatre, which has been erected on the site of the old entrance and reading rooms, is of stone and with fine elevations towards the square and St John's Road, designed in Italian Renaissance. In the centre of the principal facade is the grand entrance, with an outer balcony over leading from the Dress Circle saloon. Tall towers, terminating with domed roofs, flank the centre facade and the whole is a worthy addition to the architecture of Buxton. A glazed iron shelter at the entrance is provided to protect visitors from inclement weather upon alighting from their carriages. Polished mahogany doors, filled with brilliant cut glass, conduct the visitor to the handsome marble lined vestibule (with a beautiful painted ceiling and Mosaic marble floor) containing the grand staircase of polished white marble, with massive alabaster scrolls at the foot and marble seats at the side. Over the floor is a large Turkish carpet, and this is continued up the centre of the staircase to the crush room. A handsome apartment with the walls panelled with silk tapestries and the ceiling is rich in design. Through handsomely draped openings and short corridors the auditorium is approached on the Dress Circle level, and wide and easy staircases lead from these corridors down to the stalls on each side of the stage.' [9]

Despite the passage of nearly one hundred years, that description could apply to the theatre today. With the exception of the glass domes which once adorned the entrance to the Pavilion Gardens, very little has changed and the impact on visitors upon entering the theatre foyer for the first time remains as impressive as ever.

On May 30th 1903 the directors of the Buxton Gardens Company applied to the local magisterial bench for licences which would allow them to use the building for entertainments and to sell alcoholic beverages in the refreshment saloons. Mr T C P Gibbons was instructed by the solicitors, Bennett & Co, to appear on behalf of the applicants and a Mr Batty of Manchester represented a number of local ratepayers and property owners to oppose the application. Verbatim coverage of the application appears in the *Buxton Advertiser* and Mr Willoughby pointed out to the bench that the public had been asking for bar facilities in the existing theatre for many years. They were fully expecting the new Opera House to have a drinks licence, particularly since the building was already equipped with two saloon bars and many of the country's other theatres already had an alcohol licence. Disturbance had been caused in the past by people leaving the auditorium during a performance in the pursuit of refreshment and it was believed that facilities 'in house' could alleviate the problem. The bench, composed of JPs Mr A W Lowe (Chairman), Dr Dickson, Mr A P Shaw and Mr F Turner, were implacably opposed to the alcohol licence, believing that a drinks licence might attract the less desirable customer and lower the tone of genteel Buxton society. Coverage of the application has some amusing moments. Mr Batty (opposing) gives us such an example in his dialogue with a witness:

Mr Batty: You suggest that 51 out of every 100 complain of the want of refreshments in that place?

Witness: A majority of the young men and old have complained to me.

Chairman: You must have had a rough time of it.

Witness: If you only knew the curses that have been laid on my shoulders by these people.[10]

The magistrates retired and returned after only a few minutes' consultation to issue their verdict on the matter. The theatre was to be granted a theatrical licence strictly on the understanding that no further application should be made for an excise licence and that alcoholic beverages could not therefore be sold in the premises. And so it was that the new theatre was to open with its two new gleaming saloon bars remaining dry. This situation was to remain in place for the next twenty-five years until the theatre was finally granted a drinks licence in 1928, by which time most theatres had alcohol licences and 'a quarter of a century too late', according to the *Buxton Advertiser*.

The completed 1,200 seat theatre opened for business on June 1st 1903. The *Buxton Advertiser* reported that the theatre would probably be officially

opened by the famous actor and personal friend of Matcham, Henry Irving,[11] but for reasons unknown he was not present at the opening but did attend a performance of the play *The Eternal City* in August 1903. In the event, the Opera House opened without pomp and circumstance with a performance of *Mrs Willoughby's Kiss* by Frank Stayton. The choice of play was obviously not accidental and was probably a tribute to John and Arthur Willoughby, father and son, who both served as secretary to the Buxton Improvements Company (later Buxton Gardens Company). John Willoughby (1838-1916) came to Buxton in the late 1850s and was secretary of the company and manager of the Gardens from 1885-1903. Arthur took over the role of secretary from 1903-1912.

The theatre doors were opened a little after 7.00 pm and the foyer and stairways soon were full of first nighters anxious to view the interior of the theatre. Shortly after 7.30, carriages began to arrive and the stalls and dress circle were soon full. The play began just after 8.00, with the playing of the National Anthem conducted by Mr Herman Kiel. The curtain rose and a prologue was delivered by Miss Evelyn Aylestone before the performance began in earnest. The play was very favourably received and upon the final curtain shouts were heard from the audience demanding the appearance on stage of the manager, John Willoughby. The manager duly appeared and made a short speech in which he invited the audience to 'Charge your glasses and drink success to the new Opera House.'

Willoughby then invited the architect, Frank Matcham, on to the stage. Matcham said a few words, concluding with his good wishes for the success of the theatre.

The audience will have used this first night of entertainment as an opportunity to view the inside of the theatre for the first time and they could not fail to be impressed. The *Buxton Advertiser* gives a detailed description of the interior shortly before its opening:

> *'The theatre is built on up to date lines, and with all the latest improvements, the floors, the galleries, staircases and roof are all of concrete and iron, all passages and staircases are wide and commodious, and the exit doors are provided with Brigg's patent alarm exit bolts which prevent the doors being opened from the outside, but they give way to the slightest pres-*

sure from the inside.

A heavy fireproof curtain is provided to the stage opening, and the wall dividing the auditorium from the stage is continued up through the roof, iron doors prevent fire being carried up through the other openings. Hydrants fully equipped are provided in the most desirable positions, in fact everything has been done for the safety of the public that human ingenuity and skill can suggest.

The sanitary and ventilation matters have had careful attention, there are retiring rooms fitted with every convenience for each class of the audience; large cloak rooms, smoke rooms etc. have been provided and the comfort of the audience has had every consideration, this applies to the gallery and pit patrons equally to those in the stalls and dress circle.'

We see here an example of the class distinction which was not uncommon in the theatre at that time. Fortunately today all such social discrimination within the theatre has been largely removed, although ticket pricing policy still charges more for the 'posh' seats in the dress circle than the stalls, upper circle and gallery. The *Advertiser* goes on to describe the dress circle:

'On each side [at the top of the stairs] handsome draped openings lead into small lounges from which wide but short corridors conduct the visitors to the dress circle seats and the private boxes. Staircases at the end of these corridors are continued down to the stalls, which are furnished with thick carpet and four rows of luxurious tip-up arm seats; and these are accessible, and are divided from the orchestra by a very handsome bold brass barrier draped with silk brocade. The walls are covered with white Carrara marble, with plinths and bases of Emperors red marble.

The floors are inlaid mosaic. The ceiling is richly carved in raised plaster work, with a very fine artistic panel in the centre representing lyrical poetry, the side panels being treated with musical trophies and flowers.

From the crush room, small flights of steps lead into the rear seats of the dress circle.

The circle is fitted with comfortable, striped, velvet tip-up seats, and each seat obtains a clear and uninterrupted view of the stage and a fine view of the House...

The auditorium is particularly well provided with exits, each part having in no case less than two, and these are so well designed that the building can be cleared in three minutes.

The decorations of the auditorium are carried out from Mr Matcham's designs and are very rich; the style adopted is Louis XV1.

The ceiling is in the shape of an oval dome formed into six painted panels representing music, painting, poetry, literature, dancing and comedy; a large curve-shaped frieze joins this ceiling to the flat panelled ceiling over the stage, which contains paintings in monochrome, representing grace, strength and music.

The Buxton coat of arms, also treated in monochrome on a gold background, forms a graceful feature over the proscenium arch.

On each side of the proscenium are three private boxes, two on the dress circle level draped with light blue silk brocade and plush valances and curtains; these boxes are divided by beautiful columns of fine polished African onyx; a deep border of similar marble surrounds the stage opening, which has a deep valance corresponding with that to the boxes.

A feature is the top private boxes, caryatids support arches filled in with coved-shaped shells, and the effect is most artistic.

The fireproof curtain has been very artistically treated with a special design imitation iron grill, and

> *the drop scene, by Hemsley, has been painted to accord with the general design of the theatre.*[12]

Despite this detailed description of the theatre, no mention is made of the overall colour scheme of the interior. Fortunately the *Builder* magazine[13] tells us that the predominant colours used were blue, gold and cream. The elaborate plasterwork of the ceiling and upper walls is the work of Mr F De Jong of London, whom Matcham had used on many occasions on his other theatre interiors.

Surprising also is the lack of inclusion in the description of the ingenious gas powered ventilation system in the centre of the ceiling, known as a sunburner. The equipment consists of an array of downward facing gas jets fitted beneath an exhaust duct to the outside, and works on the theory that hot air rising from the auditorium would be vented to the outside through the ceiling. The whole process is stimulated and accelerated by the hot gas jets. This form of ventilation had been used by Matcham and other architects for many years and was thought to be an efficient way of replenishing the foul air in public buildings, although there can be no doubt that the system did nothing to stop carbon dioxide falling into the body of the theatre.[14] In order for the system to work effectively it was, of course, necessary to make vents in various parts of the theatre so that fresh air could enter from outside and replace the stale air, which was removed by the sunburner. These decorative vents can still be seen throughout the building, most noticeably in the stalls, under the dress circle balcony. The advent of electricity went some considerable way to improving air quality and it is interesting to see that the Opera House auditorium, which was never lit by gas, was nevertheless still ventilated by a sunburner.[15]

Although the *Buxton Advertiser* states that the whole theatre was lit by electricity, it fails to mention that the stage footlights or 'float' were originally lit by gas, fed from a distributor on the prompt side of the stage. The distributor could also divert gas for use in lighting the dressing rooms. The system of lighting the footlights, which had been patented in 1883, was considered to be a sophisticated version for its time and was referred to as the triple system. Earlier ignition systems had been very noisy, with the whole length of footlights being lit from a single pilot light. The triple system added another stage to the ignition process, the 'flash'. The pilot in this process lit the flash and the flash lit the rest of the footlights, thus making for a quieter and less dangerous ignition. It is likely that the gas system was only used for a short time before electricity was used for all the theatre's lighting.

The building had all the safety features of its day, with an iron fire curtain separating the stage from the auditorium so that in the event of a fire the smoke and flames could be prevented from travelling from one to the other. Matcham had lived through the period of some dreadful theatre fires which had resulted in loss of life and he took the issue of safety in his theatres very seriously. The building also had many fire exits so that the house could be evacuated quickly should it be necessary - a thing that we take for granted in public buildings today but quite an innovation for its time. In comparison with the theatre on St John's Road, the seating and sightlines at the Opera House were a great improvement. The use of cantilever engineering allowed Matcham to build the sweeping circle and upper circle without the use of large columns which would inevitably block the view of people in the stalls. [16]

So here in 1903 we have an Opera House to rival any to be found in England at the time. Would the investment optimism of the Buxton Gardens Company be handsomely rewarded?

References

1 *Buxton Advertiser,* December 28th 1901
2 Read, Jack: *Empires, Hippodromes & Palaces.* Alder man Press. London. 1985
3 Walker, Brian: *Frank Matcham, Theatre Architect.* Blackstaff Press. 1980
4 Sachs, Edwin O: *Modern Opera Houses and Theatres.* 3 vols. 1896. Benjamin Blom Inc. New York. 1968 re-issue (vol 1) p 41
5 *Buxton Advertiser,* December 28th 1901
6 *Buxton Advertiser,* May 3rd 1902
7 *Buxton Advertiser,* November 22nd 1902
8 Walker: op cit. 1980
9 *The Era.* May 23rd 1903
10 *Buxton Advertiser,* May 30th 1903
11 *Buxton Advertiser,* September 6th 1902
12 *Buxton Advertiser,* April 25th 1903
13 *The Builder.* June 13th 1903
14 Walker: op cit. 1980
15 The Concert Hall (1876) in the Pavilion Gardens is fitted with a sunburner which is unfortunately no longer visible due to the introduction of a false ceiling to the inside of the dome.
16 Read: op cit. 1985

Act One

The success of *Mrs Willoughby's Kiss* was followed the next week by the play *Little Lord Fauntleroy* by Mrs Hodgson Burnett, the playbills advertising the production as

> *'Direct from Wyndham's Theatre, London.*
> *Now playing to enormous business at the*
> *Casino Theatre, New York.'*

And the lead role was played by 'the celebrated child actor, Master Vyvian Thomas'.[1]

The first Shakespeare play to be performed on the Opera House boards was brought by the Osmond Tearle Shakespearian and Classical Repertoire Company. From July 20th-25th 1903 this company presented three plays, *The Merchant of Venice, David Garrick* and *As You Like It.* It is to be hoped that the late July weather conditions were favourable in 1903, as the playbill goes on to advertise

'Special Open Air Matinees
in the grounds adjoining the Pavilion.
SPECIAL NOTICE!
The Glees and other incidental vocal music in
'As You Like It' will be rendered by the famous
Yorkshire prize quartette, the Albion Gleesingers.
Should the weather be wet, the performances
will take place in the Opera House.'[2]

Opera was first presented at the theatre from September 14th to 16th 1903, with a visit from Mr Mouillot's Company who presented the celebrated Japanese opera *The Geisha, A Tale of a Teahouse,* with music by Sydney Jones and lyrics by Harry Greenbank. The same production, by the same company, had been given at the Pavilion Theatre on St John's Road some six years earlier, in August 1897, when the opera was relatively new.

The new facilities on offer at the Opera House meant that the Pavilion Theatre now became the Old Theatre. It continued under this name for a short time until the introduction of silent movies, when it was fitted out with projectors and screens and reopened as the Hippodrome. As the moving pictures increased in popularity, further cinema facilities were created in Buxton with the building of the Picture House (later Spa Cinema) in Spring Gardens in 1916.[3]

The local amateur groups were quick to use the facilities at the Opera House and the Buxton Amateur Operatic Society presented three performances of the comic opera *Falka,* beginning April 12th 1904. The following year the same group returned in May with a further comic opera, *Les Cloches de Corneville.* If the elaborate design of the programmes and the costumes shown in the photographs are any indication, the company was reasonably prosperous at the time and certainly went to town with these two productions.

The Opera House provided a rich mixture of plays, musicals and opera over the years immediately following its opening and initially attracted large audiences. The annual reports of the Buxton Gardens Company show that the Opera House remained in profit for the whole period of their management of the theatre. The profit made in 1904 was in excess of £1,300 but in succeeding years profits slowly declined, reaching their lowest point in 1913 when the annual working profit was less than £200. From 1913 onwards, profits rose year upon year despite the onset of the First World War (1914-1918). The annual report of the Buxton Gardens Company of March 1909 talks of the financial position of the theatre in the preceding year:

> *'Although the Opera House has been visited by superior theatrical companies to those of any previous year, the profit of £528 1s 2d is the lowest since the opening in 1903. Arrangements have been made by which smoking is now allowed in the lounges as well as in the corridor, thus obviating a continual cause of complaint, which we hope the visitors will fully appreciate.'*

Smoking policy at the Opera House during this period was somewhat haphazard, with certain productions stipulating a ban on smoking in the auditorium. Smoking was, however, generally tolerated in the theatre and this inevitably took its toll on the decoration of the interior, covering the walls and ceiling with a nicotine brown. This can, of course, be remedied with redecoration but the same sticky coating cannot be easily removed from painted picture surfaces, such as the central ceiling paintings, and these remain dull and unattractive to this day, despite conservative restorations.

A November 1911 playbill advertised a forthcoming production in what would be today regarded as a rather politically incorrect manner:

'Extra Special Attraction!
Charles Harrington's Original No 1 Great American Combination in Mrs Beecher Stowe's Beautiful Work
UNCLE TOM'S CABIN
REAL NEGROES. FULL CHORUS.'[4]

And worse still, in May 1913, when Matt Kilduff presented

'The Sequins
Soubrette - Dancer, Coon Comedian & Dancer, Pianist, Contralto, Tenor, Comedian & Child Mimic.
In a repertoire of Original Songs, Concerteds, Burlesques etc. Bright, Brisk and Breezy.'[5]

The First World War made noticeable changes to the entertainment on offer at the Opera House.

The Empire Hotel was used during the war as a discharge depot for returning Canadian troops, which brought many servicemen into the town, and the content of the programme was adjusted to cater for their tastes. Variety shows and revues dominate the bookings during the war years and programmes of 1914 repeatedly carry the announcement that 'The Opera House will be open every week during 1914.'[6] July 1914 saw

'a return visit of KINEMACOLOR in an up to date
and new entertainment, supported by
Norah Read and Tom Brown, vocalists.
Carnival at Nice (1914)
The Husband's Story - Part 1 - Drama
The Husband's Story - Part 2 - Drama
Ice Skating at Murten
British Soldiers
International Yacht Racing, Kiel
Presentation of Colours at Sandhurst
Church Parade, Aldershot
Keeping up with Hubby - part 1 - Comedy
Keeping up with Hubby - part 2 - Comedy.'[7]

The Home Office saw the theatre as a very efficient method by which to disseminate war propaganda and the Opera House was occasionally used to screen films and illustrated lectures by use of the 'Cinematograph'. In October 1917 D W Griffith's mighty spectacle *The Birth of a Nation* was screened twice daily. The advertisement boasts that

> 'The Birth of a Nation *will never be presented in any but the highest class theatres, and at prices charged for the best theatrical attractions. 18,000 people, 5,000 horses, 3,000 scenes, cost £100,000, 8 months to perfect.'*[8]

1919 was a particularly successful year financially, giving a total profit from the theatre of over £2,000. This buoyancy probably paid for the fitting of new boilers in both the Pavilion Gardens and the Opera House in 1919, which resulted in a more efficient heating system. However, the company as a whole began to experience a decline in prosperity during the 1920s as fashions changed. By 1924 the annual working profit had fallen to a little under £1,000.[9] Mr H C Sweeting (chairman of Buxton Gardens Company and Agent to the Duke of Devonshire's Buxton Estate) speaking at a public meeting on Wednesday September 21st 1927 explains:

'It is evident not only to the directors but also the public at large that this company found, in later years, considerable difficulty in carrying on. This was, without doubt, by no fault of the directors, but owing largely to the change in the taste of the general public. High class music was no longer a paying proposition, but a luxury, and a luxury which the public expect to obtain for nothing. This applies not only to the band but the Gardens as well. The same is the case in Harrogate, Bournemouth, Eastbourne or anywhere you like; you get a band for nothing and gardens for nothing. The two main propositions for the company were, therefore, cut from under their feet. What were the directors to do? Was it in the best interests of the shareholders to break the Gardens up and sell as best we could to any body, making it a godforsaken second Manchester here? Or was it better to negotiate with the Corporation? The only thing we could do was to get in touch with the Corporation, because we felt they were the proper people to run these Gardens if we could not do it ourselves.'

By the time Mr Sweeting made this speech, representatives of the Gardens Company and the Corporation had been jointly managing the Gardens and its theatres for some months, in preparation for a takeover by the local authority. The Pavilion Gardens and all properties held by the Gardens Company, including the Opera House, changed hands at this meeting and became the property of the Corporation. The total price paid to the company was £29,550 and a cheque for £10,750 was handed to Mr Sweeting by the Mayor (Councillor W Goodwin) to seal the deal. The remaining balance of £18,800 went to the debenture holders in the shape of Corporation mortgage stock. The ratepayers of Buxton thus became the new owners of the Opera House and Gardens and received a good deal, effectively paying only 30s (£1.50) for a £5 share of the old company.[10]

The Buxton Amateur Dramatic and Operatic Society, BADOS (known earlier as the Buxton Amateur Operatic Society) hired the Opera House for a three-night production of the comic opera *Tom Jones* by Edward German, beginning January 5th 1928. Later the same month the Corporation closed down their new acquisition for a week in order to reseat the auditorium. Photographs of the auditorium on early Opera House programmes show that the original layout had two aisles in the pit benches. During this reseating, the two gangways were replaced by a single central aisle and the pit benches, which had formerly been situated behind four rows of dress stalls, were replaced with red plush tip-up seats. The whole of the seating on the ground level was henceforth referred to as the stalls and was divided into front, middle and rear stalls and priced accordingly.

By the early 1930s fewer companies were prepared to bring their productions to the Opera House, as the popularity of the talking films attracted more people to the cinema than to live entertainment. BADOS continued to present its two or three annual productions at the Opera House and visiting professional companies brought their shows to the theatre for an average three-night run. One example, in October 1930, was the farce *The Chinese Bungalow*, a melodrama of the East, by Marion Osmond and James Corbet, starring George Butler as Yuan Sing (a wealthy Chinese gentleman).

Efforts were made by the Corporation to keep the theatre open for drama and musicals but in 1932 it bowed to the inevitable and the theatre was wired for sound, projectors installed and the Opera House became a cinema. This immediately brought about a situation of competition with the existing cinema, the Picture House in Spring Gardens. The Opera House cinema could boast more comfortable seats and surroundings and it is perhaps a consequence of this that the Picture House was completely rebuilt in the Art Deco style in 1937 and renamed the Spa Cinema.[11]

The Opera House programme for November 1933 offered five films:

Cynara
starring Ronald Colman and Kay Francis
The Great Jasper
with Richard Dix and Edna May Oliver
Facing the Music
Stanley Lupino and Jose Collins
Secrets
with Mary Pickford and Leslie Howard
Below the Sea
starring Fay Wray and Ralph Bellamy

Senior residents of Buxton remember the presence of a curtain which was lowered during intervals at the Opera House and was painted with a Gainsborough-type scene. It depicted an Edwardian lady in flowing gown and wide-brimmed hat sitting on a garden swing, being gently pushed by a young blond boy in pink satin pantaloons. It is likely that this curtain was the one referred to in the *Buxton Advertiser's* description of the theatre in 1903 and was in fact painted by the artist, William Hemsley.[12] A similar curtain or 'act drop', also painted by Hemsley, was discovered during the restoration of another Matcham theatre, the Gaiety, in Douglas on the Isle of Man. This has recently been carefully restored and brought back to its former glory.[13] The Buxton 'act drop' may have been used to hide the steel fire curtain which had been installed in 1932 when the projection equipment was installed. Films at the Opera House were originally back-projected on to the screen and the projection equipment was housed on the stage. The fire curtain was fitted so that the audience and stage area could be quickly separated in the case of equipment fire.

The Hippodrome on St John's Road, now no longer a cinema, became redundant once again and the building changed its name, this time to the Playhouse, and reverted to its original purpose, a theatre. The interior underwent a refurbishment in about 1936, when the walls were painted with murals. The years following the opening of the Playhouse were undoubtedly the most productive and entertaining period in the existence of the building. It was first used for music and amateur drama festivals before becoming the base for the Buxton Repertory Company, who performed drama every summer season from 1945.

The Buxton Repertory Company, under the direction of Anthony Hawtrey, featured many now famous actors. Nigel Hawthorne, Patrick Cargill, Joan Sanderson, Gwen Watford and Jos Ackland are examples of the company's regular cast members. Another member of the company, Shaun Sutton, went on to a career with BBC television, directing such programmes as *Z-Cars, The Troubleshooters, Sherlock Holmes* and *Kipling*. In 1966 he became Head of Serials and Head of BBC Television Drama Group in 1969.[14] Television in the 1930s was still in its infancy and a visit to the theatre was very popular with holidaymakers and local residents who could see a varied programme of entertainment from the same company. The work schedule for the players was extremely demanding and it was the order of the day to perform a play in the evening and rehearse for another during the daytime. The 'rep' had a hard core of dedicated followers and the company was well aware that its future depended upon this continued support. One way in which the company tried to encourage audience loyalty was a weekly competition offering two free tickets for next week's play to the member of the audience who wrote the best review of the current production.

In the 1930s and 40s it became established practice to take all the elementary schoolchildren of Buxton, Fairfield and Harpur Hill to see the annual pantomime at the Opera House. This was financed by the reigning Mayor through his or her hospitality fund and more often than not, given the total cost, was topped up at his or her own personal expense. One such visit would have been the 1946 panto *The Sleeping Beauty,* starring members of Hawtrey's company such as Patrick Cargill, Reginald Selleck and Joan Sanderson.

If I may be allowed for the final paragraph of this chapter to divert the text from historical fact to my own observations, I would like to say that, from the point of view of the historian, theatre programmes can be quite infuriating. All of them give the day and month of the production but only about fifty per cent of them give the year. This, of course, is entirely logical from the point of view of the theatre management because it was obvious to the paying public which year the show was scheduled, as the productions were only advertised a few weeks before their appearance. This leaves historians in a bit of a muddle and so it is that I have before me two programmes featuring Anthony Hawtrey's repertory company producing *Away From It All* by Val Gielgud in the week commencing September 8th and, the following week, *The Family Upstairs* by Harry Delf. The year of production is not shown but the programmes state that it was the seventh season of Anthony Hawtrey's London Company, which should date it to 1951. Both productions featured the now famous actor, Nigel Hawthorne.

References

1 Opera House Programmes. In bound volumes 1903-1930. Buxton Public Library
2 Ibid
3 Leach, John: *The Book of Buxton 1987*. Barracuda Books
4 Op cit. Opera House Programmes
5 Ibid
6 Ibid
7 Ibid
8 Ibid
9 Annual reports of Buxton Gardens Company
10 *Buxton Advertiser,* September 24th 1927
11 Leach: op cit
12 *Buxton Advertiser,* April 25th 1903
13 Friends of Gaiety Theatre, Douglas, Isle of Man: *Safeguarding the Past. Facing the Future*. Ninetieth Anniversary Appeal. 1990
14 Sutton, Shaun: *The Largest Theatre in The World.* BBC Publications. 1982

Act Two

Back at the Opera House, films continued to be shown as usual but in 1930 it was suggested that Buxton should emulate the spa town of Malvern and introduce a festival of entertainment and base it at the Opera House. The Malvern Festival had been founded in 1929 and soon established itself as an example to follow. The advice of the famous dramatist and critic, George Bernard Shaw, was sought on the possibility of founding a festival using outside professional advisers, which provoked the concise suggestion from him that 'if Buxton cannot organise its own cultural activities it must do without them.'[1]

The whole of Shaw's reply to the suggested festival is more explanatory and points out very sensibly that, in his opinion, it would be preferable to manage a festival locally rather than to bring in famous people from outside who were already overburdened with work. Despite Shaw's advice, the Corporation did go out of town to seek help and found it in the shape of Lilian Baylis, of the Old Vic Theatre, London.

Lilian Baylis (1874-1937) became manager of the Old Vic Theatre in 1912, taking over from her aunt, Emma Cons, who had opened the theatre (originally the Royal Victorian Coffee Music Hall) in 1880. Baylis went on to manage both the Old Vic and the Sadlers Wells Theatre, which was used for opera and ballet. Her parents were well known as concert party artists and their influence helped establish a deep love of theatre and music in their daughter. By all accounts Lilian (or 'The Lady' as she was often called) was a formidable figure and led the Old Vic Company with a directness that could be withering. Describing her friendship with the Baylis family, the actress Dame Sybil Thorndike recalls her first meeting with 'The Lady':

> *'I thought I must be in the middle of an explosion. Lilian rushed into her office and thundered abuse on her then director, Ben Greet, with whom I had trained and with whose company I had toured America ten years before. "What an extraordinary way of treat-*

ing the head of your theatre," I thought. Then Lilian turned to me suddenly and said, "Now you're the daughter of the clergyman, aren't you? You'll be alright then."'[2]

Baylis was a religious woman and would not think twice of turning directly to God and kneeling in prayer when she encountered difficulties with her running of the company. All existing photographs depict the unsmiling Miss Baylis as a rather sombre woman and the actor Ralph Richardson describes the good lady from his viewpoint:

'In saying that Lilian Baylis was like the moon, I do not wish to imply that in her manner she was cold. None of us felt that. On the other hand she was not sunny. She was too satirical.'[3]

One final indication of her character is given in a recollection by Alec Guinness of his first meeting with her:

'I did not actually meet her until Tyrone Guthrie had decided to take me into his company at the Vic in the 1936/37 season. He introduced me to her one morn-

ing at rehearsal. I think I must have been wearing a sports jacket and flannels at the time. Miss Baylis looked up and asked "What are your legs like?" This, apparently, was a question she frequently asked of new members of her companies. So I had to roll up my trousers and show that I actually had calves to my legs. She took a quick look and said, "That's alright. You'll do.""[4]

Lilian Baylis agreed to bring her company to Buxton in August and September 1937, before the opening of the Old Vic autumn season, and so it was that the first Buxton Festival began. The three-week festival ran from August 30th to September 18th and featured three plays: *Pygmalion* by George Bernard Shaw, *Ghosts* by Ibsen, and Shakespeare's *Measure For Measure.* Members of the company included Robert Morley, Diana Wynard, Jay Laurier, Mark Dignam and Sylvia Coleridge. The first night of *Pygmalion* was marred by a power cut, which fortunately was only of short duration, just before the beginning of the play. Light was restored to the theatre just as the theatre manager, Captain Holmes, was on stage reassuring the audience. The nonchalant crossing of a black cat across the stage footlights during the second interval seemed to augur well for the production and the play was well received by an appreciative audience. Miss Baylis addressed the well filled auditorium at the end of the show with a degree of admonishment, having noticed some empty seats at the back of the house:

> *'I don't want to see the gallery looking like this again please. It is nearly empty. Do let us have a full gallery for our season here. We love playing here and we want you to love us.'* [5]

Her schoolmarmly style seemed to have the desired effect. The gallery for the final performance of *Pygmalion* contained 206 people and the plays were packed each and every night. Total audience figures for the three-week festival were 16,167 and the festival made a total profit of £400. In addition to the plays at the Opera House, the festival held a summer school at the Playhouse, hosted by the British Drama League. In conjunction with the summer school, an extensive exhibition of models made by the staff and pupils of Buxton College was displayed in the Pavilion Gardens. A series of lectures were given at the Playhouse by the director of

Pygmalion, Tyrone Guthrie, and the director of *Ghosts,* Esme Church. Lilian Baylis gave a popular lecture on the history of the Old Vic and made clear her pride in having produced all of Shakespeare's plays at the theatre, including her least favourite, *Titus Andronicus.*

The festival was a great success and the town was filled with visitors who in turn spent their money at restaurants, shops and hotels, resulting in a significant boost to the local economy. The festival had received much press coverage, both nationally and locally, successfully putting the little town of Buxton on the map. Everyone was anxious that this prosperity should continue and at the close of the festival the Mayor, Dr W Shipton, announced the intention of the Corporation to hold a second festival in 1938 if the Governors of the Old Vic Company would agree to return. Miss Baylis was given a great ovation by the audience when she announced that they would be happy to return the following year. The company was duly booked but it was, alas, to be without Lilian Baylis, who died on Thursday 25th November at the age of 63, only two months after the festival. The national press gave great coverage of her death and many tributes were made to her dedication to the promotion of the arts and theatre. She was cremated at Golder's Green Crematorium and a memorial service was held at the church of St Martin-in-the-Fields. Buxton's own memorial to this great lady is in the shape of a plaque at the top of the Opera House main staircase which reads:

This tablet
is a tribute to
Lilian Baylis
CH, MA, LLD
and the 'Old Vic'
who did much
to advance
Dramatic Art
and to whose
inspiration and
enthusiasm the
success of the
Buxton
Theatre Festival
is largely due.
'Rosemary for Remembrance'
September 1939

The allusion to 'Rosemary for Remembrance' is taken from Ophelia's lines in *Hamlet*. It was Baylis's habit to give sprigs of white heather to the members of the Old Vic Company on the first night of a production. At Buxton and later at the Old Vic in 1937 she gave sprigs of rosemary.

Much free publicity was given to the second festival when the MP for Accrington, Major Proctor, put a question in the Commons concerning the forthcoming festival. He was concerned that the Buxton Corporation was going beyond its powers in undertaking to pay the salaries of The Old Vic Company at a cost of £2,125, the expense of transporting cast and scenery and the price of advertising the festival. He argued that the 1927 Buxton Corporation Act ruled that no cost should be made to the ratepayers from a speculative venture such as this. Proctor was opposed to municipal trading and was concerned that it might create a situation of competition with other traders in the town. The minister to whom the question was addressed, Sir Kingsley Wood, made it clear that he had no powers to interfere in the case, provoking Mr Proctor to ask for an official inquiry into the matter. In the event, the problem was overcome by the Buxton

Corporation who handed over the running of the festival to a company, High Peak Entertainments Ltd, who were lessees of the Opera House. Their opinion was that the Opera House was the only place in the town which was offering such entertainment and was therefore not in competition with any other enterprise. It is unlikely that Mr Proctor would have been very happy with the arrangements but the publicity generated by this controversy in the press for the second festival was most welcome.

1938 saw the Corporation making a significant investment in the Opera House. The profits from the previous festival must have gone some little way towards providing a new Strand Electric 'Sunset' lighting board, which gave the backstage team the ability to make several lighting changes at one time. Although purely mechanical in operation, the fader wheels on the board could be linked or 'ganged' together, so that a turn on one wheel resulted in a similar turn on another wheel on the board.

The second festival was held between August 29th and September 17th 1938 and the three plays selected were *Hamlet*, Sir Arthur Wing Pinero's

Trelawney of the Wells and *The Rivals* by R B Sheridan. The festival began with *Trelawney of the Wells,* a comedy concerning the fortunes of a theatre company in the 1860s. The next night saw *The Rivals,* produced by Esme Church, in which Ellen Compton played Mrs Malaprop, Anthony Quayle was Captain Absolute and a young actor by the name of Alec Guinness played the yokel, Bob Acres. The part of Lydia Languish was taken by Hermione Hannen and Sir Lucius O'Trigger was well played by Andrew Cruickshank (perhaps best known as Dr Cameron in *Dr Finlay's Casebook* on BBC television in the 1960s).

Tyrone Guthrie had replaced Lilian Baylis as the manager in charge of the Old Vic and it was he who produced the full unabridged version of Shakespeare's *Hamlet* in modern dress. The Prince of Denmark was played by Alec Guinness. The part of Polonius' son, Laertes, was played by Anthony Quayle and Claudius, King of Denmark, was played by Andrew Cruickshank. The unexpurgated version of *Hamlet* lasted three hours, forty minutes and in order for the production to finish at a reasonable time the curtain rose nightly at 6.40 pm. An interval of forty minutes was provided in the middle of this marathon performance so that the audience could take dinner in the surrounding restaurants and hotels. This inevitably caused some complaint from those who were forced to rush their meal in order to return to the theatre for the continuation of the performance. For all these inconveniences, the play was very well received and remarks were made that, despite its great length, the play was not considered to be wearisome or exhausting. The use of modern dress by the cast had been of concern to many who felt that the lack of period dress might take some of the colour out of the show but the generally held opinion seemed to be that the overall effect, using a combination of court dress, military uniform and evening dress, was a success.

A review by Vernon Noble in the *Daily Express* described Guinness' performance:

> *'There is nothing unconventional about Alec Guinness' Hamlet but there was more unearthly beauty about his diction than I have seen in almost any other Hamlet. Not a line was lost, not a movement without significance. A fine sophisticated performance given its four hours entirety.'*

The *Advertiser* carried a small review by 'Jay':

> *'The Hamlet of Mr Guinness will rank as one of the great Hamlets of our time. It was first of all great as a feat of memory, great from the reality of his work. He was well inside the part. It used to be said of Aynsley Cook that he did not play Devils-Hoof: he was Devils-Hoof. So also with Mr Guinness' Hamlet: he was Hamlet. His beautiful delivery of the magnificent lines is a lesson in elocution.'*[6]

The hon secretary of the festival, Mr J E Boddington, reported to the *Advertiser* at the end of the festival that, although the event had begun well and played to full houses, the last week had not shown a repeat of the last week of the first festival. He admitted that in retrospect the choice of a 6.40 pm beginning for *Hamlet* had been a mistake and had probably resulted in excluding people from attending who would otherwise have done so. He also expressed his disappointment at the level of local support and stated that the apathy and criticism shown by many Buxtonians would cause the company to give very careful consideration to the advisability of holding another festival the following year.[7]

The announcement in May 1939 of the third Buxton festival was welcome news. The four-week event featured the plays *Romeo and Juliet* by William Shakespeare, *Viceroy Sarah* by Norman Ginsbury, *The Devil's Disciple* by George Bernard Shaw and *The Good Natured Man* by Oliver Goldsmith. The cast list contains probably the most famous names to attend any of the festivals. Robert Donat, Constance Cummings, Stewart Granger, Andrew Cruickshank, Andre Morrell and Ernest Hare all appeared at the Opera House. The first play, *Romeo and Juliet,* opened on August 28th, with Robert Donat playing Romeo and Constance Cummings as Juliet. The opening performance of *Viceroy Sarah* took place the following day and *The Devil's Disciple* successfully completed its first performance on the 31st. The festival got off to a roaring start, with the 'house full' board in evidence every night, and optimism abounded when suddenly it was brought to an abrupt and unwelcome halt.

Concern about the deepening crisis in Europe had been on the minds of many over the preceding months and the threat of war had to be considered when making plans for any public occasions. War was declared against Germany on September 3rd

Romeo and Juliet

by

WILLIAM SHAKESPEARE

★ *CHARACTERS IN ORDER OF THEIR APPEARANCE* ★

Chorus	Andrew Cruickshank
Sampson	James Hoyle
Gregory	Thomas Heathcote
Abraham	Ninian Brodie
Balthaser	Anthony Compton
Benvolio	Manning Whiley
Tybalt	Stewart Granger
Capulet	Ernest Hare
Lady Capulet	Sonia Dresdel
Montague	Robertson Davies
Lady Montague	Sophie Ellis
Escalus	Willoughby Gray
Romeo	Robert Donat
Paris	Basil Coleman
Page to Paris	Daniel Thorndike
Peter	Max Adrian
Nurse	Marie Ney
Juliet	Constance Cummings
Mercutio	Andre Morell
Friar Laurence	Hubert Harben
An Apothecary	Andrew Cruickshank
Friar John	Ninian Brodie

From the Third Buxton Festival programme
August 28th to September 23rd 1939

1939 and the festival was immediately halted. The Home Office invoked emergency regulations which resulted in the suspension of the operations of all theatres, cinemas and other places of entertainment. Although this was a blow to the festival, the secretary, Mr J E Boddington, was confident that as Buxton was officially classified as a 'non-vulnerable' area, the ban would be lifted after application to the Home Office. The Old Vic Company remained in Buxton until a reply to the town's exemption application was received. Permission to continue was granted a few days later and the festival started again on Saturday September 9th. Certain regulations were imposed, however, which stipulated that no names in lights should be displayed outside the theatre and the house should be empty by 10.00 pm. New performance times were announced, with evening shows beginning at 5.30 pm and matinees on Wednesdays, Thursdays and Saturdays at 1.45 pm.[8]

On the last day of the festival, Saturday September 23rd 1939, Robert Donat unveiled the plaque to Lilian Baylis. Donat's speech recalled an occasion which shows that, despite her apparent severity, Lilian Baylis had a lighter side to her nature:

'Her sense of humour never wavered, even when she was run over by a bus in London, someone looked under the bus and exclaimed that it was Lilian Baylis of the Old Vic. Nobody thought she was still alive but a voice was heard to say from under the bus, "and the Sadlers Wells too."'[9]

Later that evening, after the final performance of *A Good Natured Man,* the Mayor of Buxton made a speech from the stage, saying, 'In spite of the general blackout I think you will agree that Buxton has been favoured with brilliant stars shining each night in this theatre' and concluded by expressing the hope that permanent peace would be established long before the next festival was due.[10]

We now know, of course, that the Mayor's hope was a forlorn one but the war did not deprive Buxton of a fourth festival. All other festivals throughout the country had been abandoned and Buxton was therefore unique in being able to continue with its programme of entertainment. This time the festival was shortened, beginning on August 15th 1940 and ending only nine days later on August 24th, and presented only two plays, Goldsmith's *She Stoops to Conquer* and *The World Is Yours* by the Spanish dramatist, Gregorio Martinez Sierra. The festival organisers had been very careful, expecting small turnouts given the anticipated difficulties of war-time travelling, but audiences exceeded all hopes, with large numbers of people attending from other towns. The restrictions of the previous year's festival were at least partially lifted and all the plays were advertised at the normal starting times of 8.15 pm and 2.30 pm.[11]

However, the war was beginning to affect theatre audiences and although there was a fifth festival in 1941 it was a small affair compared to its predecessors. It ran for one week only, beginning on August 11th. *King John* by Shakespeare was the chosen play and the lead part was played by Ernest Milton, Dame Sybil Thorndike playing the part of Constance. One matinee performance of the play *Medea* by Euripides was performed on the Thursday. An indication of the falling interest can be clearly seen in the August issues of the *Advertiser* which carry only a fraction of the coverage given to the previous festivals.

The sixth and final Buxton Theatre Festival took place in 1942 from June 22nd to July 11th. *Jacob's Ladder* by Lawrence Housman took up the first week, and the remainder of the festival was devoted to three Shakespeare plays, *Othello, The Merry Wives of Windsor* and *The Merchant of Venice*. The decline in interest in the festival, first shown in the previous year, continued and it is with a degree of bewilderment that the *Buxton Advertiser* of July 4th 1942 reports in its editorial:

> *'Mr Boddington and his fellow promoters of the Old Vic Festival were very disappointed with the patronage extended to the performances this season. In the previous festival great enthusiasm has been shown and our opinion was that with such a list of attractions we should create a record. Even Jacob's Ladder with Dame Sybil Thorndike and Lewis Cassell in the cast did not play to anything like capacity and this week the houses have been alarming. To our mind there could not have been a more attractive bill of Shakespeare plays than is offered this week. We are quite conscious that there are transport difficulties and weather to contend with but this should not affect local play goers to such an extent as has been apparent this week. There is still a week in which to make amends and we appeal for greater support from lovers of the stage lest we sacrifice our festival and*

deprive ourselves of the only three weeks of drama in twelve months.'

The appeal for greater support fell on deaf ears and, as with so many things that begin with much celebration and pomp, the Buxton Festival ended with a fizzle rather than a bang. The following Monday saw the Opera House back to showing films as if nothing had happened, with

'South Of Suez'
Starring George Brent, Brenda Marshall, George Tobias
Women untamed! Dangers Unknown! Men Unafraid!

For many years following the demise of the theatre festival, the Opera House continued to operate as a cinema and live entertainment remained on offer at the Playhouse. The showing of films at the Opera House was occasionally suspended when the local amateur theatrical companies presented a show there and also when the annual pantomime came to town. The short-lived professional Drama Festival may have ceased to function but Buxton was not to be denied drama, or indeed drama festivals, as the next chapter will tell.

References

1 Postcard from George Bernard Shaw to Mr R J Finnemore dated August 19th 1936
2 Souvenir Programme of the Lilian Baylis Centenary Festival 1974. Opera House Archive
3 Ibid
4 Ibid
5 *Buxton Advertiser,* September 4th 1937
6 *Buxton Advertiser,* September 10th 1938
7 *Buxton Advertiser,* September 17th 1938
8 *Buxton Advertiser,* September 9th & 16th 1939
9 Letter (undated) from Mildred Winterbotham. Opera House Archive.
10 *Buxton Advertiser,* September 30th 1939
11 *Buxton Advertiser,* August 24th 1940

Act Three

Of all the companies who played in the town we must never forget the contribution made by the local amateur talent. Buxton was fortunate in having more than three separate amateur companies and all of them performed at both the Playhouse and the Opera House.

The Buxton Amateur Dramatic and Operatic Society (BADOS) was formed in 1902, being an amalgamation of the Buxton Operatic Society (formed 1898) and the Buxton Dramatic Society (formed before 1892). The company gave a musical and a dramatic performance practically every year, with the exception of the periods of the two World Wars. In 1945, after the last war, a group of former members joined together to reform the society, raising funds by holding dances, competitions, etc, and finally succeeded in raising enough money to stage the musical comedy *Over She Goes* in 1946. The following year the company staged *Sporting Love* and in 1948 *The Desert Song*.

The Buxton Opera Group had its origins in the Buxton Festival Group, which had formed in the Festival of Britain year, 1951, in order to contribute to the local celebrations. Members were drawn from amateur societies, churches and choral groups in the area. Two local residents, Hugh Skeens and Paul Askew, wrote and composed a new opera with ballet sequences called *Ann Tregenna* and the Festival Group gave six performances of the show at the Opera House in September 1951. This production aroused a great deal of public interest and enthusiasm amongst those taking part, leading to the formation of a self-supporting body, the Buxton Opera Group in 1952. The first production to be staged by the group was *Merrie England* in October 1952.

The third theatrical group, the Buxton branch of the British Drama League, was formed in 1922. Their first play, *Bazhouka meets the Gods* by F Sladen-Smith, was performed in the ballroom of the Buxton Hydropathic Hotel on Hartington Road. The group presented their first production at the Opera House in 1924. The society staged on average three productions annually, consisting of a major three-act play, a members' evening of three one-act plays for the less experienced and an entry in the local drama festival held at the Playhouse. No plays were attempted by the league during the years 1940-1947. The first play to be staged after the war, entitled *Grand National Night,* was at the Playhouse in 1948 and the society adopted the name 'Buxton Drama League' in 1961.

Buxton Townswomen's Guild also had a drama section and, whilst the Guild existed to serve other purposes, the small drama section was an enthusiastic group who presented many plays in Buxton. For many years the group produced an excellent pantomime, which inevitably included many local interest references. The pantomines were written and produced by local solicitor, Graham Beadle.

Amateur companies from the north of England came to the Playhouse to compete in the drama festivals, which were organised by the Buxton Corporation. The annual festivals began in 1936 and consisted of a week of one-act plays in April and a further week of full length plays in November. The plays in both cases were adjudicated independently and marks were allotted to the companies for acting, production, stage presentation and dramatic endeavour. The adjudicator presented a judgment every night on stage after the performance and the audience was encouraged to give its own ratings as the festival progressed. The theatre archive contains a number of festival programmes and it is obvious from the pencilled numbers inside many of them that the audience was involved with the adjudication. The winners of all the categories were presented with an award at the end of the festival.

The festival was suspended in 1939 and recommenced after the war in 1949. Some years later, a combination of lack of interest and finance caused the Corporation to pull out and the festival was taken over by a small group of devotees, including Charles Clowes, Rona Bowden, Kay Beadle and May Arnett. The Corporation offered the group the use of a room, a typewriter and remaining petty cash and it was on such shaky ground that the volunteers took on the future of the festival. After 1960, separate full-length and one-act festivals were merged into a single event held annually in the spring. This small but enthusiastic team maintained the festivals over the following years and linked the Buxton performances to similar events throughout the country by joining the National Drama Festivals Association (NDFA) when it was formed in 1964. When the popularity of the one-act festival dwindled, it was decided to drop the one-act plays and continue using full-length productions only.

Anthony Hawtrey's repertory company, which had given so much entertainment to a dedicated audience, wound up its operations in Buxton in the early 1950s and was almost immediately replaced by another professional repertory company, the Penguin Players. From 1956 until at least 1959 this company brought its productions to the Playhouse. A glance at the Penguin's programmes shows that they did not go in for anything particularly ambitious or deep-meaning but served a wholesome programme of thrillers, comedies, farces and whodunits. The fact that this company came to Buxton every year and performed many shows suggests that they were popular. Those who remember the company recall that a leading member of the team had a noticeably stiff leg, which must have affected his credibility when trying to act many different roles as part of the repertory team!

A proud boast announced on their programmes that:

The PENGUIN PLAYERS
now have companies playing at
BEXHILL-ON-SEA
EASTBOURNE
TUNBRIDGE WELLS
CLACTON-ON-SEA
PETERBOROUGH
MORECAMBE
SHEFFIELD
and
BUXTON

Amongst the many plays they produced during the years in Buxton were *Separate Tables* by Terence Rattigan, *Spider's Web* by Agatha Christie and *Dry Rot,* a farce by John Chapman.

At the Opera House a packed house was assured on December 17th 1953, when Sir Edmund Hillary delivered an illustrated lecture on his recent successful conquest of Mount Everest. Hillary was introduced by Jack Longland, Director of Education for Derbyshire County Council and a former Everest mountaineer. Much interest was shown in his lecture and the reaching of the summit, which was announced to the world almost simultaneously with the coronation of Queen Elizabeth II. At the end of the lecture a vote of thanks was given from the stage by the present (eleventh) Duke of Devonshire.

In 1957 the Buxton Opera Group staged a world premiere at the Opera House of a musical entitled *Passion Flower*. The music for the show was based on Bizet's *Carmen* and the lead parts were played by Elizabeth Harwood (Micaela) and William McCue (Escamillo), both of whom went on to become world famous opera singers.

Financial problems in the Pavilion Gardens complex led to some difficult decisions at the Borough Council meetings. Savings had to be made to keep the business viable and the decision by the local authority in 1970 to close down the Playhouse and put it in 'moth balls' caused great consternation amongst the local amateur theatrical societies who presented many of their shows there.[1] During an Opera Group rehearsal of *Orpheus in the Underworld* in 1971 the cast discovered that a large hole had been made between two of the Playhouse dressing rooms and the adjoining kitchens at the Pavilion Gardens. The Council had decided to convert two of the seven dressing rooms into a still

BUXTON OPERA GROUP

room for the Gardens kitchens and, without further consultation, had made a start on the work. Leading members of the Opera Group and BADOS organised a protest meeting at the Palace Hotel in March 1971, which resulted in the formation of the Buxton Playhouse Theatre Association whose purpose was to investigate the means by which it could take over the running of the Playhouse. The degree of opposition to the Council scheme caused suspension of the building work pending debate in the council chamber which, by all accounts, was rather animated.

During the discussions which followed between the Council and the Playhouse Association it was suggested and eventually agreed that the running of the theatre be taken over by a limited company of interested people.[2] The Buxton Theatre and Arts Trust Ltd was thus formed and a series of negotiations with the Council eventually agreed the terms by which the Trust could take over the theatre. The local authority agreed to rent the building to the Trust for an annual rent of £10, providing certain conditions were agreed to. Catering facilities for the theatre remained the responsibility of the authority and would be provided by the Pavilion Gardens staff. The Council retained the right to use the theatre during the daytime for conferences and associated functions. A further stipulation was that for twenty-one days of the year they would have the use of the theatre for council supported events, such as the regular Old Time Music Hall Shows which had been held in the theatre for some time. These terms were agreed upon by all sides and in November 1972 a short ceremony involving the handing over of a symbolic key sealed the deal. The theatre officially passed to the Trust and came under the care and protection of those who had a strong vested interest in its survival.

The Playhouse now became the centre of live entertainment in Buxton and, although it had fewer facilities than the Opera House, it had a small and intimate auditorium with reasonably comfortable seating in the stalls and circle. The dressing rooms, which were housed under the stage level were, to say the least, small and were woefully inadequate to accommodate the cast of a reasonably large production. Despite these restrictions, the theatre was used for a wide range of productions and somehow even the most complicated shows, with large cast lists, were performed in the theatre. The Playhouse was reopened on February 7th 1973 with the Yorkshire Theatre Company presenting Wesker's *Four Seasons* and *Ballet for All* by dancers from the Royal Ballet. May 1973 saw opera in the Playhouse, when the London Opera Centre gave a performance of Gounod's *Faust* and followed it the next evening with Mozart's comic opera *Don Giovanni*.

A summer season of plays was presented by professional companies at the Playhouse from 1974-1979 with a grant from the Council on an eight-week repertoire basis. These were greatly appreciated by summer visitors to the town. The interval catering for these plays continued to be provided by the Council but in 1976 it was taken over by a lady member of the Trust. This set a precedent for the use of volunteers to provide front of house services and help with fundraising, which was transferred in 1979 to the Opera House and is still very much in operation today.

References

1 *Buxton Advertiser,* April 3rd 1970
2 *Buxton Advertiser,* September 24th 1971

Finale

Continued use of the Opera House as a cinema, with no investment in its infrastructure, resulted in deterioration of the interior. By the 1970s, the effects of water ingress through the ageing and uncared-for roof were evident in the damp walls and peeling wallpaper. The amateur company, BADOS, performed *Oklahoma* there in October 1976 and at the end of the one-week run the theatre was closed to the public until the following spring. An inspection of the auditorium and backstage area was carried out during the closure and it was anticipated that some urgent work would need to be undertaken to make the theatre fit for public use again. It was at that time held on lease from the High Peak Borough Council by Buxton and High Peak Entertainments Ltd, part of the Hutchinson Leisure Group of Burnley, for a mere £1,250 per annum. Neither the cinema company nor the Council were inclined to find the money necessary to renovate the property and the situation was further complicated by the fact that the theatre was listed as a building of special architectural interest. Cheaper renovation approaches which might be used were therefore not appropriate in this case. Hutchinson's lease on the property was due to expire in 1981 and the company could not justify the necessary expenditure, given the short time remaining. It had felt for some that time the building failed to meet its requirements as a cinema, being cold and in need of refurbishment. This was having an effect on attendances and thus the quality of films they could lease to show.

The cinema company and the Council entered into discussions, with the aim of overcoming the problem, and sufficient work was performed on the theatre's structure to allow it to be reopened in April 1977 with the highly popular film *King Kong*. The Hutchinson Group subsequently announced its intention to extend the lease beyond its expiry in 1981 and, by bricking up the proscenium arch (stage opening), proposed to divide the building into two studios showing separate films, thereby increasing choice for the public and profit for the company.

At about this time, the theatre had taken the interest of Malcolm Fraser of the Manchester Royal School of Music who was in Buxton for a family outing. The possibility of presenting an opera festival at the theatre seemed to him too attractive an opportunity to miss and he contacted the chairman of the Borough Council Amenities Committee, Ray Walter, to organise a tour of the theatre interior. An inspection was duly arranged and, being impressed with what he saw, Fraser proceeded with his vision to hold an opera festival in the building, following a major restoration of the theatre. The idea was met with some scepticism in the Council chamber but eventually the enthusiasm of a minority won through and the project was given a guarded go-ahead. The problem of reclaiming the lease on the property was an obstruction to the project but this was eventually overcome when the Council threatened to impose a legal order on the cinema company requiring it to renovate the interior of the building to comply with modern regulations. Hutchinson's decided that the cost of such work would be prohibitive and gave up the lease of the building early in 1978, leaving the way clear for the restoration.[1]

The London architectural practice, Arup Associates, had submitted a report and cost study for the restoration work in November 1977 which concluded that the building, although in a poor state of decoration, was essentially in good condition and could be restored to its original grandeur providing sufficient money could be found. In order to bring the theatre up to acceptable standards, they felt that the heating system with its oil-fired boiler would need to be replaced as the distribution pipework was leaking badly and was not large enough to cope with modern heating demands. All the electrical circuits in the building needed replacement and a complete rewiring would provide an opportunity to install a modern three-phase electrical supply to the backstage area. The building had no fire alarm or detection system and modern regulations insisted that such a system would need to be installed. The system of natural ventilation aided by the central sunburner in the roof was considered inadequate for today's needs and they recommended that an electrically operated system of ventilation should be installed, although it was recognised that the noise levels created by such a system could be intrusive. The biggest recommendation from the Arup report was that the existing orchestra pit was inadequate and needed to be enlarged. They suggested the creation of a larger understage pit to accommodate the bigger orchestras used by today's operas. This was to be done by extending the stage forwards into the auditorium and creating an 'apron' stage. All this work, plus a general redecoration of the whole building and tasteful cleaning and restoration of the ceiling paintings, meant that a great deal needed to be done if the theatre was to be ready for its planned reopening at the end of July 1979.[2]

The Amenities Committee of the Borough Council persuaded the Council to form a trust to run the theatre. In fact two boards were created: first, the Buxton Opera House Trust to oversee the restoration and subsequent running of the theatre and, second, Buxton Festival Ltd which would control the Opera Festival. The estimated cost of the restoration was £509,000 and a public appeal, 'Operation Opera House', was initiated to raise the required cash and was primed by its first donation of £1,000 from the Duke of Devonshire. Sizeable grants were received from various bodies, which went a long way towards the appeal target, and donations from the public and local organisations soon raised enough money to begin the restoration work. The call for funds was given further support by a visit in 1978 by the Poet Laureate, Sir John Betjeman, a man who was keenly interested in Britain's architectural heritage. Betjeman had been invited to the town by the Duke of Devonshire for a private tour of the Opera House and declared himself 'thrilled' by the theatre's splendour. Arup Associates were appointed to design and oversee the work in 1978 and the restoration began in January 1979, with the firm of Bovis chosen as the principal contractors. This was not the first time that Arup Associates had been involved with the restoration of a Matcham theatre. In 1975 the company had extended the stage of the Theatre Royal, Glasgow, making room for a larger orchestra pit. This project would have undoubtedly given them valuable experience which could be put to good use at Buxton.[3]

Original plans of the building were unearthed and it was discovered that, despite the passage of time, the theatre interior had been changed very little and the only significant intrusion was the projection room built at the back of the upper circle. In order to achieve the enlarged orchestra pit, considerable excavation was necessary, which disturbed a spring in the area and necessitated its capping. The spring still flows today and a pump works continually to remove the water. Without this pump the lower levels of the orchestra pit would be under water. Steel beams were installed which supported the stage using cantilever principles, preserving the original stage structure with its raking, an essential requirement in ensuring good sightlines from all parts of the theatre. The excavated understage area could now house an orchestra of eighty and additional space was made available for storage areas, etc.

On the stage level, an extended area could be added to the front of the stage when the orchestra pit was not in use by inserting sections of stage to form an apron, thus extending the acting area some distance in front of the main curtain. It was originally intended that the forestage (as it became called) could be installed mechanically but a lack of funds necessitated the manual installation and removal of the apron, a very heavy task which is not relished by the stage crew. The sightlines of the original stage were so finely designed by Matcham that the extended forestage cannot be seen from parts of the auditorium and visiting actors are advised to use the area as little as possible for that reason. Despite the precise sightlining of the stage from most of the auditorium, there are certain areas which have always had a restricted view. The boxes on both sides of the theatre give a view of little over one half of the stage area and the bench seats at the sides of the upper circle can be rather uncomfortable and offer a restricted view of the stage. The box office staff are aware of these problems and will only sell these seats after customers have had the situation fully explained to them.

Lighting positions were created on bars at the upper circle level, which significantly increased lighting levels on the stage. The Strand 'Sunset' lighting board was reconditioned and left in position behind the stage but facilities were created whereby the lighting channels could be plugged into a modern memory lighting control board, should a visiting company choose to bring their own lighting mixer. Decorative, Edwardian-style light fittings were installed throughout the auditorium and other public areas. The heating system was improved but the original Art Nouveau style radiators were retained. The cherubs and caryatids which adorn the marble proscenium arch were restored and cleaned. It has been discovered since the restoration that the pillars of the boxes nearest the stage, despite being painted, are also made of marble and it is to be hoped that any future redecoration reveals this.

We have seen that the original colour scheme of the auditorium was a mixture of blue, cream and gold. An ideal restoration would have returned the theatre to its original colours but a lack of cash to replace the main stage curtain resulted in the blue being dropped and replaced with brown to match the curtain. A lucky find in one of the boxes uncovered a piece of the original 1903 carpeting buried beneath layers of more modern floor covering. The pattern was copied by the makers of the original, Firth's of Brighouse, Yorkshire, and the present auditorium carpet was woven on a 1907 loom, specially brought back into use for this purpose.

Financial constraints did not allow for the installation of a modern ventilation system but an important component of Matcham's original 'natural' ventilation device, the gas-fired sunburner by Halton's of Manchester, was restored to its original splendour. The sunburner in the centre of the auditorium ceiling was restored free of charge by a team of North West Gas engineers, who modified it so that it can be used with natural gas. During much of the time that the building had been used as a cinema, the sunburner had been treated as if it were just another part of the ceiling and had been painted blue, so as to blend in. The engineers had to completely dismantle the whole apparatus and replace the slender gas-carrying stems. The cleaning of the vitreous enamel parts, like much else, had to be done painstakingly by hand. Recapturing the period effect with scalloped gas flames similar to the old manufactured gas flame was achieved by using bat wing design burners with bray jets.[4] The burner still remains in good working order and on occasions is lit during a performance using an electrical ignition system installed during the restoration, a far cry from the days when the lamplighter leaned from the 'gods' and used a long pole with a lighted meths-soaked rag on the end.[5]

Lack of resources did not allow for the replacement backstage of the hemp flying system with a more modern and mechanised arrangement and the business of flying scenery and cloths remains today a job calling for much muscle. The timber grid over the stage, flying galleries and crossover bridges were found to be in remarkably good order considering their size (forty-two-foot lengths of six inch by one foot solid timber) and age. Winches have since been installed on the fly floor to assist with lifting the more heavy lighting bars, which would have taken several men to raise into position using the old manual system. The original safety curtain was left in place but its lifting mechanism was completely overhauled and smoke seals were fitted at the sides where none previously existed.[6]

The public bars in the building were not altered to any great degree. The most ornate of them, the Dress Circle Bar, was very sumptuous in 1903. It was at that time called the Grand Foyer and had leather wallcoverings, Turkey carpet, mirrors, old prints on the walls and luxurious chairs and sofas. Once again cash shortages dictated that the bar should be decorated in a more simple manner and, even if it were affordable, the anticipated numbers of clients using the bar ruled out the use of large furniture which took so much precious floor space. Despite the simple treatment, the Dress Circle Bar still retains an air of its previous elegance with its long mahogany bar backed by Edwardian mirrored shelves. The bar can be experienced at its best when the theatre is not too full on a balmy summer's evening, standing at the open balcony windows overlooking the Square and nursing a gin and tonic. The Stalls Bar is of very simple design in comparison and was hardly changed at all in the restoration, being very functional but hopelessly inadequate for the numbers of people who wish to take advantage of the facilities today.

Much of the Art Nouveau stained glass which adorns the building is original and that which had been damaged was brought back in the restoration. On either side of the upper circle are examples of this glasswork, with circular windows topped with raised plasterwork and gold leaf decoration. When the building was first built these windows were functional and were opened every morning to help rid the theatre of the stale air left from the previous evening's performance. The restoration kept these windows for their decorative charm but they are no longer functional. In front of these windows on both sides of the theatre are standing areas, fronted by curving balustrades topped with handrails which were sensitively restored and are today one of the prettiest parts of the theatre. The Art Nouveau

OPERA HOUSE

movement is also evident in the glass canopy outside the main entrance which indicates the separate entrances for the theatre's seating areas. Surprisingly, this glasswork has escaped any serious vandalism over the years, although a reversing van recently destroyed the middle section. The damaged metalwork was repaired by the local firm, Leander Architectural Ltd of Dove Holes, and the glasswork was restored using most of the existing glass by Cheshire Stained Glass Ltd. During this work it was noted that the metalwork had been altered at some time in its history and this can be seen to be the case by referring to early photographs of the theatre which show the canopy with a triangular iron and glass 'pediment' on top of the verandah. Interestingly, a recent piece of renovation at St Martin's Theatre, London (home of the long running play *The Mousetrap*) has introduced Art Nouveau style glasswork into a new verandah based on that at Buxton and designed by local architectural engineer, Trevor Gilman.

Externally, apart from making the roof watertight, very little was done. The remains of the neon lights which adorned the frontage during its time as a cinema were removed and new external light fittings, more in character with the building, were fitted. The exterior of the building may be described as rugged rather than delicate but its appearance fits in well with the rest of the town's architecture.

In the entrance foyer, the ice cream kiosk which had operated in the cinema years was removed. The box office at the right hand side of the foyer was extended to occupy the whole of the space which had previously been shared by the box office and cloakroom. The large expanses of white marble which now delight the eye were uncovered from beneath layers of brown wallpaper. A new metal handrail was installed on the staircase leading up from the foyer in order to conform with modern safety regulations. These stairs were originally open with a handrail on both sides and were covered by a red Turkey carpet and white linen drugget.

Operation Opera House failed to raise enough money to reach the appeal target figure and it was left to the Borough Council to find the additional finance. After much controversy, it was eventually agreed to use money from the Council's reserves in order to complete the restoration. In total, the Council made a contribution of £105,000 and donations from the public amounted to £264,000.

Donations of £50,000 from the English Tourist Board, £62,000 from the Historic Building Council and £22,000 from the Arts Council of England brought the grand total raised for the restoration to £503,000.[7]

The project was completed on time and the newly restored Opera House was ready to receive its very first audience for the opening night of the Festival Opera on 30th July 1979. A project which had seemed to many to be virtually impossible had been carried out without major hitches. The same, however, could not be said about the first night of the Festival!

References

1 *Buxton Advertiser*, November 17 1977
2 Arup Associates Report & Cost Study, November 1977
3 Walker: op cit
4 *Buxton Advertiser*, July 28 1979
5 Arup Associates. Buxton Opera House. Pamphlet. Undated. Opera House Archive
6 Ibid
7 Figures from Mr L P McCarthy, Borough Treasurer's Department and Michael Williams MB, Vice-Chairman of the High Peak Theatre Trust

Encore

Disaster struck at 11.00 am on 30th July, the first day of the first Buxton Opera Festival. Monica Pick-Hieronomi, the leading soprano of the opera *Lucia di Lammermoor* by Donizetti fell ill with tonsillitis and, at a stroke, the whole event came under threat of failure. Frantic phone calling managed to locate an American soprano, Deborah Cook, of the Bavarian State Opera, who had knowledge of the part. She agreed to stand in at short notice but was at the time in her home in Munich. By midday she was boarding a plane for Manchester, where she was met and driven to Buxton with a police escort. No time was wasted and the transfer from the airport was used to discuss staging details with the opera's assistant producer, Robert Carson. Miss Cook had performed the role of *Lucia* on several occasions but was only conversant with the more commonly performed abbreviated version of the work. The cast at Buxton had been rehearsing for many weeks on the full, uncut opera and in these final hours Malcolm Fraser (director) and Anthony Hose (musical director) had to find a way of combining the two versions into a satisfactory compromise. The soprano arrived at the theatre scarcely one hour before the curtain was due to rise.[1]

Whilst frantic last minute arrangements and rehearsals were taking place inside the theatre, people were beginning to arrive to witness the first night spectacle. As it should be (but so very rarely is in Buxton) the weather was dry, sunny and warm and from early evening the crowds began to congregate outside. Appearances on the balcony of trumpeters from the orchestra, who gave a series of short fanfares, added to the magic of the event. The air of anticipation was palpable and made more so when the news began to permeate about the lead soprano's illness. Dignitaries arrived, including the patron of the Opera House, the Duke of Devonshire, and the guest of honour, Princess Alice, Duchess of Gloucester. A short ceremony took place involving the unveiling of a plaque to mark the occasion and the audience then filtered into the auditorium to take their seats for the performance.

The Manchester Camerata, conducted by Anthony Hose, played the overture and the curtain rose to reveal the impressive opening scene with a set designed by Roger Butlin, costumes by Fay Conway and lighting by Nick Chelton. Given the circumstances, although Deborah Cook was of smaller stature physically and vocally than the planned prima donna, the performance was hailed by all as a triumph. The replacement soprano posed a headache for the follow spot operator, who had rehearsed his movements with the more rotund Monica Pick-Hieronomi, and had to adapt his technique drastically to keep track on the considerably smaller and more nimble Miss Cook.

The first night opera was followed by an impressive and very loud firework display which woke much of the population of the town, many of whom were unaware of the existence of the Festival. For days after the event locals were still pondering the source of the mighty nocturnal explosions which had untimely raised them from their slumber!

Newspaper reviews over the following days were almost all complimentary and all pointed out the bravery of Deborah Cook, who faced a full audience at the Opera House with no rehearsal and no knowledge of the other members of the cast. Miss Cook performed the part for two more nights but Monica Pick-Hieronomi recovered her voice in the middle of the first week of the Festival and sang in all the remaining performances of the uncut opera.

The whole Festival was based on the theme of the writings of Sir Walter Scott and a dramatic adaptation of his life was performed at the theatre with the actor, Fulton MacKay (more popularly known as prison warder, Mr Mackay, in the comedy TV series *Porridge*) playing the part of Scott. In addition to the opera, the Bristol Old Vic Company gave six performances of the George Farquhar play *The Recruiting Officer* before moving on to the Edinburgh Festival.

As with most major arts festivals, the Buxton Festival established a 'fringe' consisting of a programme of events dispersed throughout the town. Hotels, public houses and streets were all used as venues for these events, which ranged from plays, recitals, musicals and poetry readings to dance. The fringe continues today and although it is not on the scale of Edinburgh, it successfully entertains many visitors and residents who find themselves

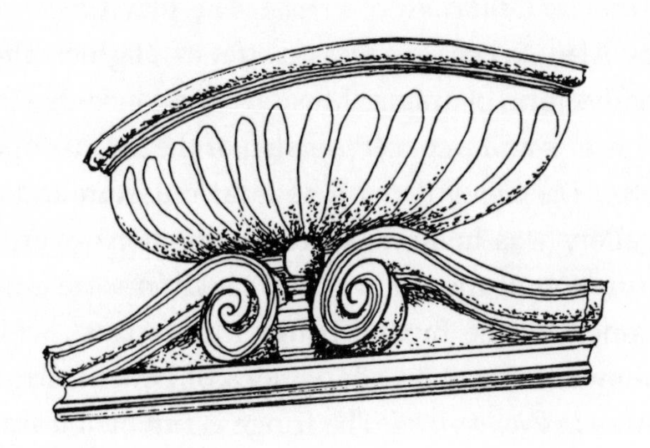

at a loose end in the evenings. Fringe events for the 1998 Festival included outdoor performances of two Shakespeare plays, *A Midsummer Night's Dream* and *The Two Gentlemen of Verona*. The play *Confusions* by Alan Ayckbourn was on offer as a lighter, alternative form of drama. Musical events included folk concerts and a concert version of the Strauss operetta, *The Gypsy Baron*. The local museum and art gallery was home to several exhibitions over the duration of the Festival and children were entertained by the Buxton fringe film festival, which showed video film adaptations of Lewis Carroll's *Alice in Wonderland*. The fringe is run by a team of local volunteers and information for all the activities can be found at the fringe information desk in the Pavilion Gardens.

The local amateur groups now had luxurious facilities in which they could present their shows. Reduced hire charges offered by the Opera House enabled them to tread the hallowed boards and all took advantage of the new theatre facilities. All three main groups presented a show in the first year of the reopened theatre. In October 1979 Buxton Drama League staged an Agatha Christie thriller, *The Hollow*. Later the same month BADOS performed the popular Lionel Bart musical *Oliver!* and in November Buxton Opera Group presented *The Gypsy Baron* by Johann Strauss. For the amateurs, facilities on offer at the Opera House, compared to the cramped conditions to which they had grown accustomed at the Playhouse, took some time to adjust to. Some, indeed, never did get used to it and to this day many look fondly back to the days of the Playhouse with its 'cosy' atmosphere.

The reopening of the Opera House put once again into doubt the future of the Playhouse. It was not viable to run the two theatres together and the Council began to look into alternative uses for the building. An overspill use to house conferences and exhibitions and generally augment the facilities at the Pavilion Gardens was generally thought to be the most appropriate.[2] Alternative suggestions included an indoor roller skating rink and a stage for minority art groups but in the end it was decided to convert the Playhouse into a multi-purpose hall with the flexibility to serve several functions and thus increase its potential to make profit for the Gardens complex.[3] A suggestion to brick up the stage opening and use the stage for storage purposes was thankfully not carried out but the stage rake (slope) had to be levelled so that functions which spilt over on to the stage could be catered for. All the lighting and backstage equipment was removed, together with the auditorium seating, leaving a large floor area which could be used for dances and gatherings of all descriptions. The circle was blocked off during the conversion and the ceiling lowered to the level of the circle floor, giving a more intimate impression than if the ceiling had been left at its original height. A bar was installed near the entrance of the hall and the facility was opened with a new name, the Paxton Suite, in May 1980.[4]

The second Buxton Opera Festival in 1980 featured two operas: *Hamlet* by the French composer, Ambroise Thomas, and *Beatrice and Benedict* by Berlioz, adapted from Shakespeare's *Much Ado about Nothing*. *Hamlet* starred the famous baritone, Thomas Allen, and was directed by Malcolm Fraser. Beatrice and Benedict were played by Ann Murray and Philip Langridge and the opera was directed by Ronald Eyre. As with the previous year, there were many other events on offer, including music, art, films and lectures. The Festival fringe which had been established during the first year expanded its programme and entertainments of a varied nature were to be seen in virtually every public building in the town. Once again, the Festival was warmly received by the critics and the public but a financial crisis which nobody had anticipated very nearly put a stop to the event.

News of an impending cash crisis broke just before the last performance of *Hamlet*. Actors, technicians and stage hands were warned that the financial position put a question mark over their wages and subsequent discussions resulted in the curtain rising twenty minutes late for the performance, which was being recorded by the BBC. The threat of no wages galvanised the backstage staff into action and they made their feelings known by refusing to move the scenery in preparation for the children's opera *Cinderella,* which was due to start at 11.00 am the next day. A petition was drawn up by the actors and technicians and was presented to the Festival chairman, David Rigby, drawing attention to certain doubts they had about the internal organisation of the Festival. Urgent talks took place between the Festival Board, Derbyshire County Council, High Peak Borough Council and the Festival's bankers, Williams & Glyn's, which resulted in the event being brought back from the brink of financial disaster. The County and Borough Councils agreed to modify the guarantees that they had previously made with the Festival Committee, which enabled the event to continue and formed a more secure base upon which all future festivals could build. One of the criticisms made during the financial crisis was that the ticket prices were too high and, as a result, all the £15 tickets for evening opera performances were reduced to £5 for the remainder of the Festival. The Festival continued after the crisis and the second opera, *Beatrice and Benedict,* attracted full houses and was warmly received.[5]

The near collapse of the second Festival was effective in concentrating minds on the financial security of the event. In the midst of the crisis a new chairman of the Festival Board was appointed to replace the outgoing David Rigby. The new chairman, David Hunter, took over at a critical point in the theatre's history but fortunately managed to turn around the fortunes of the Festival from a loss situation in 1980 to a position of surplus by 1982. This turnaround was achieved largely by the enlistment of increasing numbers of sponsors to offer subsidy.

From the reopening of the Opera House in 1979, the Derbyshire County Council provided an annual grant which went some appreciable way towards its upkeep. The relationship between the County Council and the Opera House was somewhat fragile, however, and a halving of this grant in 1982, followed by a further halving the next year, left the theatre in desperate need of funds. The County Council justified the grant reductions by stating that the Festival Board and the Opera House Boards needed to be completely separated. It felt that monies given by the Council were being directed away from the Opera House to the Festival which, it felt, served an elitist minority. Once again the High Peak Borough Council threw a lifeline to the theatre with financial aid to tide it along and before long the County Council funding ceased completely. In December 1983 the Opera House Trust was renamed the High Peak Theatre Trust Ltd, due to the High Peak Borough Council's agreement to take on more responsibility. Subsequently a greater number of borough councillors sat on the theatre's board of management.[6]

The amateur full-length play festivals, which had been staged at the Playhouse since 1936, moved into the Opera House after the restoration. The festivals usually occupied the last two weekends in June and continued with the tradition of a nightly on-stage adjudication after each performance, culminating in the presentation of various awards at the end of the festival. Companies came from all over England to compete in the event and often incurred great expense in the transportation of their scenery to Buxton. Understandably, they looked to the Buxton Play Festival Committee to defray some of this expenditure but the finances of the committee could rarely live up to this and it was a basic lack of money, together with dwindling audiences, which eventually caused the demise of the festival. The last drama festival was held at the Opera House in 1991 and the committee and festival were dissolved in 1992, with all remaining monies held by the committee being donated to the National Drama Festivals Association (NDFA). The committee was called out of retirement in 1994 to organise the twenty-first NDFA British 'All Winners' Festival at the Opera House, which was sponsored by the Derbyshire Building Society. This festival worked on the same principle as its predecessors but in this case the winning plays of each individual festival competed. The standard of production was extremely high but, although audiences at the beginning were reasonable, the intervention of a rail strike severely affected attendances from those who came to Buxton using public transport. Attendances dwindled alarmingly during the second weekend of the event, which went some way to justify the decision made by the committee to terminate the local festival in 1992.

The success of the Opera House restoration created casualties amongst the local amateur theatrical groups. Although lower rental rates were levied on the local groups, the cost of staging musical shows at the Opera House spelt the end for BADOS and Buxton Opera Group. Enthusiasm amongst both groups remained high but, as with many local societies, fewer and fewer younger people were joining the groups and if their financial plight had not led to their demise, the slow ageing of both groups would most certainly have. BADOS performed at the Opera House for the last time in 1983 with the musical *Annie Get Your Gun,* although they continued to produce concerts elsewhere for a short while in order to pay off their remaining debts. Buxton Opera Group's swan song was *Oliver!* in

April 1987, after which the group was officially wound up and all remaining funds donated to the Opera House. Of the three main amateur groups only one, Buxton Drama League, still remains active. The league still presents three productions a year, although not all at the Opera House.

The traditional annual Christmas pantomime was provided at the restored Opera House by an amalgamation of various members of the local amateur societies under the banner of the Buxton Theatre and Arts Trust. It will be remembered that the Theatre and Arts Trust was formed in 1972 to take over the running of the Playhouse from the Council and, although by this time the Playhouse was no longer in use as a theatre, the name of the Trust was still used in connection with the pantomime. The Trust was effectively brought to an end when it was decided in 1988 to institute a professional pantomime with a longer run than that which could be provided by local players. Although the amateur version was popular, the professional pantos which have been held every year since then have been a great attraction and form an important part of the theatre's income.

The Opera House has been used by television companies since the restoration as a venue for concert recordings or as a film set in its own right. The rental of the theatre to the media has been an important source of income, as the final chapter recalls.

References

1 *The Guardian,* August 1st 1979
2 *Buxton Advertiser,* September 20th 1979
3 *Buxton Advertiser,* November 1st 1979
4 *Buxton Advertiser,* May 22nd 1980
5 *Buxton Advertiser,* August 4th 1980
6 McCoola, Ros: *Theatre in the Hills.* 2nd edition. 1994. Caron Publications

The Show Must Go On

The comedy duo, Hinge and Bracket, were amongst the first to have their television series recorded on the Opera House stage. Mike Harding, the Rochdale comedian, recorded at least one of his shows there and has appeared at the theatre several times since. The recording of a short television film called *God Rot Tunbridge Wells* inside and outside the theatre gave local amateurs the chance to dress up in Georgian wigs and frock coats. The addition of a curly wig and beauty spot can alter one's appearance quite dramatically and much mirth was displayed by the extras when, one by one, friends emerged from the make-up room transformed into a 'beau'. Sir Laurence Olivier appeared on the boards of the Opera House during the Granada television filming of J B Priestley's *Lost Empires* in November 1985. The television company took over the theatre for three weeks whilst the filming took place. The BBC uses it as a venue to broadcast the biennial Sainsbury's *Choir of the Year* contest.

Since the reopening of the Opera House, a wide variety of types of entertainment have been housed there, including musicals, plays, comedians, magicians, puppet shows and one man comedy shows. Some have been memorable, some less so, and a few of these are worthy of mention. For sheer ambition, Buxton Drama League must be applauded for its production of *Dr Who and the Seven Keys to Domesday*. The show's director, Geoff Lunn, is a man not easily put off by the daunting scale of producing a show of this complexity and excelled during the preparation for this production. Together with other members of the league, he constructed six full-size daleks which were big enough to house a child inside so that the thing could be guided. Castors underneath the machine enabled the person inside to propel it around the stage but the whole was very difficult to manoeuvre, given the combined problems of restricted vision and the slope of the raked stage. The first appearance of the daleks on stage with their distorted electronic voices made a big impression on the audience but the effect soon fell flat when one of the daleks ran out of control and became trapped on the forestage in front of the curtain. The sound of a weeping and claustrophobic dalek operator could be clearly heard from this stranded enemy of the human race and did little to reinforce the reputation of the daleks as the masters of the universe![1]

Around the World in Eighty Days, a musical directed by Robin Ray, presented its world premiere at the Opera House in June 1990. Destined for the West End of London, the show, starring Anthony Head (of the Gold Blend TV advertisement fame) opened with a blaze of publicity and the launch of two *Phileas Fogg* hot air balloons from the adjoining Pavilion Gardens. The show was felt by most people not to live up to expectations and disappeared into obscurity after its Buxton premiere. Unlike its title, it failed not only to circle the globe but also to reach its hoped-for London destination, although the show was performed at the Liverpool Playhouse in the following year.

The *Quest For New Musicals* was an ambitious project launched by the theatre administrator, Chris Grady, in 1990. The Quest was given financial support from British Nuclear Fuels and 491 new musicals were received, of which 150 were assessed by a professional panel, with Andrew Lloyd Webber as patron. In Easter 1992 the Quest had been narrowed down to two musicals which received workshop performances, playing to producers, critics and the public. Despite much effort and other supporting events, the Quest failed and showed a deficit of £43,000, moving the theatre as close as it has ever been to liquidation since its reopening.[2]

A visit by the Russian Ice Stars to the theatre in June 1996 to perform *The Phantom of the Opera on Ice* presented the company with what appeared to the layman to be the huge logistical problem of levelling the stage rake so that a frozen lake could be created on stage. The company was obviously well rehearsed in the erection of the refrigerating unit and the theatre was converted to the purpose in a very short time. Because of the levelling of the rake, the front of the frozen skating area was inevitably considerably higher than the normal stage level and visibility from the stalls was somewhat restricted. For those in the stalls, and as a consequence at a much lower level than the skaters, the prospect of a player leaving the rink and flying into the auditorium was deemed a very real one as they appeared to glide precariously close to the front edge.

A show by the comedians, Hale and Pace, in May 1990 was interrupted by a bomb hoax alert which necessitated the rapid evacuation of the theatre. In the true tradition of British comedy the show went on and the duo continued their performance standing on the wall of the Old Clubhouse public house until the auditorium had been searched and the audience was allowed to return.

The comedian and theatre historian, Roy Hudd, gave a memorable four-night run of *Roy Hudd's Music Hall* in November 1981. Hudd has a great knowledge of and love for the British music hall and its performers. Using his talent for mimicry, he gave portrayals of the old stars of the halls, including Max Miller, Dan Leno, Billy Bennett and many others.

Ken Dodd has appeared at the theatre on numerous occasions, never failing to pack the house for his comedy shows which are notorious for their late finishes. A recent visit filled the house from 7.30 pm to well after midnight on both nights!

In addition to the annual Opera Festival, the theatre plays host to visiting opera companies throughout the year. The Milan Opera Company have presented several shows in Buxton, the most recent being *Un Ballo in Maschero* by Verdi in March 1996. Ballet is also on offer throughout the year and London City Ballet are amongst the theatre's regular visitors.

A wide selection of plays are presented at the theatre by touring drama companies, including Compass and Bridge Theatre. Productions range from serious works by Shakespeare and Ibsen to comedies by John Godber and Mike Harding.

The decision to open the Opera House to the international Gilbert & Sullivan Festival for two weeks in 1994, immediately following the main Opera Festival, was an inspired one and the festival of competing amateur companies was an immediate success. The event, now in its fifth year and directed by the indefatigable Ian Smith, has increased in popularity almost to the point of being a serious rival to the Opera Festival itself. The organisers and competing casts have an infectious love for the Savoy operettas which is conveyed to the visiting audiences and the atmosphere in and around the theatre is noticeably turned up one notch during the period of the festival.

The organisers of this event staged the First International Musical Theatre Festival, immediately following the G & S Festival in August 1997. This is intended to become an annual event and the 1998 festival included *Fiddler on the Roof, Annie, Chess* and *The Sound of Music* amongst many others.

Backstage at the Opera House, the Strand Sunset mechanical lighting board was used for a short time after the reopening but was hopelessly inadequate for the lighting plots demanded by the technical staff and visiting companies. In 1981, the stopgap installation of a CRD (choke reactance dimming) lighting board helped the technicians along until a new modern system could be purchased. The CRD board had seen previous service at the ABC Theatre, Blackpool, and was operational at the Opera House until 1983 when a Strand Duet 2 multi-channel computerised system was installed. The old Sunset unit, by this time something of a rarity, was traded in to Ancient Lights, a television props company, in return for ten acting area lanterns, items which were sorely needed in the early days of the theatre's reopening. The old board, or parts of it, has been seen in various films and plays since then, including Ronald Harwood's *The Dresser* and Priestley's *Lost Empires*. The latter was partially filmed at the Opera House in 1985 and the Sunset unit was brought back, somewhat ironically, to be used as a prop in the very theatre where it had served for so long.

In 1990 the Duet board was replaced with a Gemini 2 Plus, the current lighting console, again supplied by the Strand Lighting Company. The association with Strand has been of benefit to both the company and the Opera House. The firm uses the theatre on a regular basis to train its staff and gives payment to the Opera House in the form of stage lanterns. This arrangement has resulted in a healthy collection of lanterns within the theatre, which in turn helps reduce costs incurred by the regular hire charges for such equipment.

The installation of a hearing loop around the auditorium has helped the hard of hearing to enjoy the productions and even the profoundly deaf can enjoy the signed performances which employ the talents of sign linguists who stand at the side of the stage and translate the dialogue of the performance into hand signs.

The main stage curtains or 'tabs' were replaced in 1995 with the present green and gold curtain and the drapes in the boxes were changed at the same time for a matching green material. Way above stage level, in the fly gallery, little has changed and the scenery and lighting bars are still raised and lowered using the original rope and pulley systems. Simple, non-sustainable winches had been installed in 1939 while the building was in use as a cinema but these were replaced in 1985 with safer sustainable winches. The replacement winches contain ratchets which do not allow the cable to wind back off the winch roller when the handle is at rest.

The original asbestos fire curtain was operated by a hand crank and it will be remembered by the many who have tried to lift it without stopping through its total of sixty-two turns. It was replaced in 1994 with a double-sided fibreglass and steel curtain which can be operated electrically. The rails which fronted the orchestra pit are no longer used during musicals and operas as it is felt that they are not substantial enough to hold back a crowd of people in the case of an emergency, when a surge to the front of the auditorium might occur. The pit rails are not original and were fitted during the restoration. Instead, the wooden frontage of the apron stage is left in place, which is far more substantial and does not affect the acoustical quality of the orchestra.

No theatre can operate without an efficient system of ticket sales to the public. For several years after the restoration, the box office continued to use the manual system of ticket distribution, based on pads of books with tear-off tickets, which many of us will remember. The introduction of a computerised system, PASS, which was installed in January 1990 at a cost of £44,000, revolutionised the method of ticket sales. The advent of the new technology still allows for tickets to be booked in person at the box office but also by telephone, post, fax, e-mail and via many out-of-town ticket agents. The system is also used to keep regular theatre-goers informed of the forthcoming programme and, by acquiring their post codes on the computer's database, to create audits and thereby analyse the audiences received for all kinds of shows. Statistics acquired from the system are used by the theatre's publicity and marketing staff to target each show as effectively as possible.

Although the Opera House is, to all intents and purposes, a professional theatre, it differs from many in that virtually all of the front of house staff are volunteers. With the exception of the front of house manager, all the staff who tear tickets, serve drinks at the bar and show you to your seats do so without remuneration. As we have seen, this tradition was established whilst the Playhouse was operating as the main theatre and was passed on to the Opera House after the restoration. Immediately after the reopening and for many years following, the staffing rota was organised by the stalwart honorary house manager, Bob Burrows, and his wife Nora. Sadly, Bob died in 1988 and the front of house manager became a paid post, currently filled by Martin Robinson, who frequently doubles as a choreographer for certain productions, most notably the annual pantomime.

The importance of volunteer house staff cannot be overemphasised in this precious little theatre. The finances of the Opera House are such that it could not possibly operate if it were forced to pay these people and we are lucky that so many are prepared to give up so much of their free time to keep the theatre alive. Training is given to all staff in how to evacuate the theatre in case of fire quickly and efficiently. Another group of enthusiastic volunteers, the Friends of the Opera House, organise coffee mornings at the Opera House every Saturday morning, amongst other fundraising activities.

The theatre historian and former archivist of the Opera House, Ros McCoola, established the Willoughby Luncheon Club in 1983 in order to raise funds for the theatre. The club was formed for people who live outside Buxton and was named after John and Arthur Willoughby, whose involvement in both the Pavilion Gardens and the Opera House has been covered earlier in this book. During its existence the Willoughby Club has raised significant amounts towards the theatre and has financed the purchase of many articles of equipment.

At present, the theatre can only rely on one regular source of income in the form of an annual grant from the High Peak Borough Council, which this year (1998-9) stands at £43,000. All other revenue has to be generated by ticket sales. The last financial year (1997-8) showed a financial surplus and it is to be hoped that the great financial crises suffered by the theatre during its early years are a thing of the past. Although it is still necessary to sell raffle tickets during the intervals in order to raise funds, it is hoped that there will be no return to the days when the front of house staff had to hold buckets at the exits, inviting departing audiences to empty their pockets of loose change. Thanks to the dedication of the staff, the board and in particular the recently retired theatre manager, Judith Christian, the theatre now hosts more performances per year than ever before and achieves an average annual audience capacity of fifty per cent, a most respectable figure for any provincial theatre in the land. The range of entertainment on offer is now probably more varied than at any other time since its reopening and still attracts audiences from a wide catchment area.

Despite the 1979 restoration, the Opera House is in desperate need of investment if it is to continue to operate as a theatre far into the twenty-first century. The figure of £503,000 which was raised to restore it pales into insignificance in comparison to the amount of money needed to bring it up to modern day standards. Many millions of pounds will be needed to carry out this work and, like so many others, the Opera House has applied for National Lottery funding. A first bid to the fund, made in March 1998, was unsuccessful and the hopes of the theatre's future lie heavily on a successful second bid. Amongst the work that needs to be done is the construction of new offices and public toilets, and improvement of the backstage area, including the installation of a pit lift to help with the transport of large items of scenery and equipment into and out of the theatre. The back-stage dressing rooms, which are currently in a sorry state, need much renovation and redecoration. New seating is needed in the auditorium and the gallery, where there are only benches at the moment. Improved access for the disabled will necessitate the removal of some of the seats in the stalls, reducing the total seating capacity from its present 937. The theatre bars, which at the moment are inadequate for the numbers attending, need to be extended and thus increase the revenue from drink sales to the theatre.

1998 saw the twentieth Buxton Opera Festival, featuring the opera *La Finta Semplice* by Mozart and *Eugene Onegin* by Tchaikovsky, and the Festival was as artistically successful as many of its predecessors. Once again a financial crisis, caused by the withdrawal of an expected £15,000 grant from the Arts Council, very nearly resulted in the collapse of the Festival but it was saved at the last minute by a massive injection of cash from the Derby based company, Williams plc.[3] The Festival was immediately succeeded by the highly popular Gilbert &

Sullivan Festival and was followed into autumn by the usual varied mixture of drama, dance and musical.

To those who feel that the future of theatre in Buxton, and particularly the Opera House, must be ensured and improved upon in the years to come, the idea of failure through lack of finance or for other reasons is almost inconceivable. The town of Buxton has had a theatre for the greater part of 200 years, beginning with a 'mean' building in Spring Gardens in the middle of the eighteenth century. We now have one of the most beautiful theatres in the country but still cannot take for granted that this wonderful palace of entertainment will remain and prosper by itself. Much dedication and work will be needed to keep the theatre alive in Buxton, particularly in an age where theatre attendances amongst the younger generations appear to be in decline. The future of the Opera House is difficult to predict but the hard work put in by so many people over such a long period must surely mean that it will remain healthy and continue to provide high quality live entertainment in the town for a long time to come. As the theatre nears its centenary in 2003 may we all wish that the years ahead will bring us an ever improving theatre. Buxton deserves no less.

References

1 For those unacquainted with daleks, they were an alien and distinctly antisocial species who used a mechanised transporter, not unlike a dustbin, as their life-support system when invading other planets. They were first brought to our attention in the 1960s in the BBC television series *Dr Who*.
2 McCoola: op cit
3 *Buxton Advertiser,* March 11th 1998

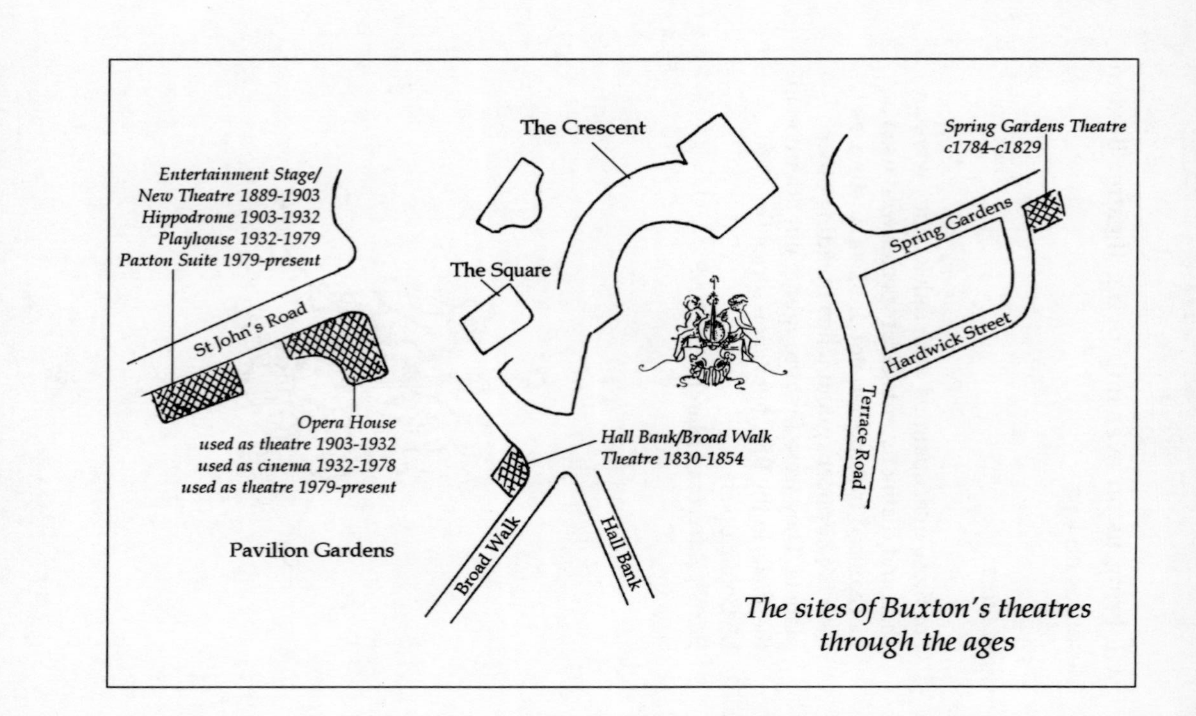

The sites of Buxton's theatres through the ages

Acknowledgements

My thanks go to many people who have helped me produce this book. Firstly, to the late Ros McCoola, whom I have not generally referenced independently in the text but whose book *Theatre in the Hills* is a source of information which could not possibly be ignored by anyone researching Buxton's theatre history. As with all the previous publications with which I have been involved, my friends and fellow local historians, Oliver Gomersal and Mike Langham, have critically read several chapters before submission to the publishers. Another good friend, Robert Cooke, has proved to be an important source of knowledge about the history of Buxton Opera Group and the Playhouse. I am grateful for the help and remembrances of Charles Clowes and Ray Walter, whose knowledge of and love for the theatre is widely acknowledged. Judith Christian, until recently general manager of the

Opera House, and other employees of the theatre have been most helpful in providing information about theatre operations since the restoration. David Marsden has supplied much valuable technical information, particularly in the field of stage lighting. Architectural detail on various aspects of changes at the Opera House has been contributed by Trevor Gilman. Figures for the cost of the 1979 Opera House restoration were supplied by Mr L P McCarthy of the Borough Treasurer's Department in collaboration with Michael Williams, Vice-Chairman of the High Peak Theatre Trust. Sue Parker kindly helped me with the proof reading of the final manuscript. As usual, the staff at Buxton Library and Buxton Museum have offered every assistance. Finally, I thank Vivien Cripps and Millrace who have provided the means by which my floppy computer disk is converted into a book. To all these I convey my sincere thanks.

CW, 1998

Appendix 1

High Peak Theatre Trust Ltd
Chairman: Margaret Millican MBE
Vice-chairman: Michael Williams MBE
Secretary: Patrick Brady
Financial Manager: Graham Sisson
Councillor J Hallsworth
Councillor K E Savage
Councillor I D Watts
Howard Barker
Robert Mullholland
C F Hughes
Clive Beattie
Mrs J R Allan
Mr G A Simmonds

Opera House Staff
Theatre Director: Andrew Aughton
Secretary: Pat Russell
House Manager: Martin Robinson
Technical Manager: Guy Dunk
Marketing Manager: Helen Dunnett
Marketing Officer: Catherine Twite
Financial Controller: Dorothy Setford

Housekeeper: Sally Marshall
Box Office Manager: Chris Nelson
Box Office Clerks: Jenny Blake, Hayley Barton, Pat Plant, Dorothy Wells, Barbara Robson
Technician: Sue Ryder
Electricians: Mark McNeill, Rob Oliver
Publicity Assistants: Lucilla Marsden, Ellen Outram, Vivienne Tyler, Mike Scholes, Joan Doughty, Valerie Richardson
Marketing Assistant: Karen Compton
Stage Door Keepers: Richard Walsh, Roy Pickles, David Howat, Heather Norton
Maintenance: Derek Gray
Cleaners: Mo Warrington, Margaret Slack, Lynda Garlick, Julie Anthony
Cellarman: Peter Barlow

Administrators and managers of the Opera House since the 1979 restoration

1979-1984
Christopher Baron (joint manager of the Opera House and administrator of the Buxton Festival.)
1984-1985
Vanessa Hart, followed by Neil Duncan (assistant manager, Judith Christian)
1985-1992
Christopher Grady (theatre administrator)
1985 to September 1998
Judith Christian (theatre manager)
September 1998 onwards
Andrew Aughton (theatre director)

Appendix 2

Opera House Front of House Volunteers

Janet Allan
Aileen Allsop
Scott Allsop
Joyce Allwright
Audrey Ashton
Barbara Baldwin
Cherry Billing
Margaret Booth
Enid Bowman
Jenny & Simon Bradbury
Yvonne Broady
Helen Burgess
Hilary Butler
Ann Challis
Dorothy Chapman
Christine Clark
John & Judith Clegg
Di Cockram
Sylvia Collis
Jackie Corrigan
Valerie Coulter
Janet Crawley
Andrew Cummings
Betty Darrah
Enid & Francis Dickson
Ruth & Eric Downs
Sue Edwards
May Forder
Mary Forsdike
Debra Franke
Fay Fraser
Dorothy Freeman
Alan & Margaret Gibson
Ann Grabowski
Angela Grice
Muriel Hallam
Pam & Katy Hallam
Bron Hebblethwaite
Paula Hobdey
Joyce Holden
Joyce Hopwood
Brenda Howard

Bob & Evelyn Huddart
Sylvia Isted
Bess Jones
Dorothy Kennett
Joan Kent
Beryl Kerr
Neil Kidd
Enid Leech
Margaret Lendon
Ann Livesley
Thomas Lowe
Geoff Lunn
Helen MacBain
Sheila Macdonald
Joan Marsden
Cynthia Martin
Pauline Massey
Ann Maxim
Pauline May
Eileen Mee
Marjorie Melling
Bea Millward
Sue Moss
Mary Murphy
Philip Nadin
Megan Owen
Bernard Peacher
Roy Pickles
Cora Plant
Daphne Roberts
Kath Rogers
Peter Rolland
Isobel Sacco
Dot Saintey
Margaret Schofield
David Scott
Stephen Shipley
Avril Spencer
Bill Stead
Brenda Stockton
Janet Stockton
Ann & Geoff Strudwick
Stella Thompson
Anna & Christine Thwaites
Rose Van Den Akker Ledger
Muriel Ward
Vera Wheatley
Margaret Wilby
Harriet Wild
Glen Wilkins
Barbara Wilson
David Winstanley
Betty Wood
Jean Wyld
Bunty Wynn Jones